THE
CROSS
AND THE
GRAIL

The CROSS AND The GRAIL

esoteric christianity
for the 21st century

Robert Ellwood

A publication supported by
THE KERN FOUNDATION

Quest Books
Theosophical Publishing House

Wheaton, Illinois ◆ Chennai (Madras), India

The Theosophical Publishing House
P.O. Box 270
Wheaton, IL 60189-0270

A publication of the Theosophical Publishing House, a department of the Theosophical Society in America

Library of Congress Cataloging-in-Publication Data

Ellwood, Robert S.
    The cross and the grail: esoteric Christianity for the 21st century / Robert Ellwood -- 1st Quest ed.
       p.   cm
    "A publication supported by the Kern Foundation."
    Includes bibliographical references.
    ISBN 0-8356-0760-7
    1. Christianity--Miscellanea.   2. Theosophy.   3. Grail.
I. Title
BR126.E52   1997
289.9--dc21   97-18843
                                      CIP

6 5 4 3 2 1 * 97 98 99 00 01 02

Printed in the United States of America

CONTENTS

PREFACE

As the second millennium after Christ draws to an end, a new interest in esoteric interpretations of Christianity is arising. The inward paths associated with that ancient faith have acquired new travelers. Christians of many backgrounds visit monasteries of the venerable Eastern Orthodox church, known for its mystical approaches to the faith. In the West, books on the Holy Grail, long recognized as having profound esoteric associations with the church, continue to stream from presses. A yearning for something that is not unchristian, yet is wider and deeper than conventional presentations of the faith, seems to be in the air.

By esotericism is meant timeless wisdom embedded, for those with the vision to see it, in the forms of a faith which outwardly appears conditioned by history and circumstance. The fundamental esoteric premise is that all spirituality ultimately is walking the Path on which every human, knowingly or not, is a pilgrim. That is the Path back to our final and eternal home from which, before the very beginning of time, we set out as adventurers seeking to experience all planes of being but sometimes forgetting our heritage. The Path home winds its way through countless worlds, eons, and life-forms. The outward forms taken by the spirituality the Path calls for in particular times and places may thus be less than absolute, though these forms may be the path within the Path to which we are absolutely called in a specific time and place.

This book is dedicated to those for whom the present windings of their path have intersected with Christianity, as they have for me. *The Cross and the Grail* and what these two symbols represent is intended for those who feel drawn to a spiritual life in which symbols and language associated with esoteric, Theosophical, and allegorical interpretations of the Old and New Testaments, and of the Mysteries of the Christian faith, are emphasized. This approach also employs motifs from the world of medieval romance, especially the quest for the Holy Grail, finding in them themes that, interpreted mystically, can be of great power in motivating and guiding those on our spiritual path. The nineteenth-century clergyman Stopford Brooke proposed that "Christianity is the most romantic of all religions"; this book is designed to appeal to those for whom this is a strong and dynamic consideration.

Esoteric Christianity is based on the premise that our lives in this world are meant to be spent in pilgrimage on the Path leading us back toward God and the Halls of Light which are our eternal heartland. Like the Prodigal Son in the parable, we have left our true home to seek a far country, but as we tire of eating its "husks" we are led to arise and go to our Father, who is prepared to greet us with festival and song. On the course of the journey home we encounter many barriers, trials, and wonders with which we must deal with all the faith and wisdom we can gather.

On our great pilgrimage those in harmony with this way of journeying will be aided by the spirit of romance, which above all holds that sublime images and imagination (literally, the making of images), conjoined with exalted feelings, are powerful guides to precede us on our Path, even as the cloud and the pillar of flame went before the Israelites in the wilderness. Of the images of romance, those from the distant past and those with the mysterious but compelling overtones of myth and archetype have the greatest power. For some people today, images from the medieval world of wondrous story, idealized though their picture of what that world may be, have a particular potency. This path will probably appeal not only to those who have been stirred by Scripture and the romance of the Grail, but also to those whose vision of Christianity has been affected by contemporary tales in the mode of medieval romance, such as Hermann Hesse's *The Journey to the East*, C.S. Lewis' Narnian stories, J.R.R. Tolkien's *The Lord of the Rings*, and the *Star Wars* trilogy of movies.

A few notes regarding the symbols of Cross and Grail will help on the journey through this book. Keeping the Cross before our eyes as we travel reminds us that, following the example of Jesus, we journey not through this world only, but through the valley of the shadow of death, into the land of the spirits in prison and past the place of the skull (Golgotha). We must die with Christ and rise with him. The Cross tells us that the Christian path is a way of death and transfiguration and that before its end, we ourselves must be crucified and rise from the tomb, in whatever form those awesome initiations take in our own lives. The Cross also reminds us that on this journey we are definitely within the Christian tradition, for the Cross is Christianity's pre-eminent symbol. Jesus the Christ, Son of God and Savior of the World, is the supreme example and guide of those on this way; he is the "great shepherd of the sheep and bishop of our souls." We honor and respect all other religious paths which make up the great Path, for we know that they also have been established by teachers of the timeless wisdom in forms suitable to their times and places, and they are also of universal validity. But we ourselves are most drawn to the way of Christ: his Cross, his mysteries, and his glory.

The Grail of medieval Arthurian and Christian romance reminds us that the Path is also a great quest for the holy, for that which will transform us and the world. There are many versions of the Grail story. It is not my purpose here to sort them out, and in the end the Holy Grail means something unique to each sincere seeker of the hidden and eternal treasure it represents. However, in one way or another, the narratives generally tell of a knight who journeys to a blighted land, perhaps ruled over by a maimed king. Reaching the country's center, the knight dares to enter a castle containing as its great treasure a chalice of imperishable brightness which is guarded by knights and maidens bearing enigmatic tokens, such as a broken sword or a lance dripping blood. The puzzling question, "Whom does the Grail serve?" must be asked by the knight in order to transform himself and restore the wasteland. In all versions there is a feeling of magical and dreamlike strangeness, suggesting that the story is ultimately about initiation and a transformation taking place inwardly, at the deepest levels of consciousness from which come dream and inspiration.[1]

This way of looking at the Grail legends is comparable to the esoteric view of religion. Without denying the historicity of many events described in Scripture and commemorated in the annual festivals of the Christian faith, our view is that their true importance is as empowering myths and allegories of experiences which we all, in our own way, must undergo: experiences of suffering and redemption, of seeking and finding, of contending with demons within, and of finding hidden gold. This spiritual and intrapsychic view of the symbols of the faith is in line with the methods of such great interpreters of Scripture as Philo Judaeus, Origen, the Gnostics, Gregory of Nyssa, the Kabbalists, Swedenborg, and Theosophists such as C.W. Leadbeater and Geoffrey Hodson. It is also similar to the inner reading of myth by such scholars as C.G. Jung and Joseph Campbell. Thus, the Exodus of the Children of Israel out of Egypt and across the Red Sea is not only a historical event; it is also an eternal sign of the progress of all souls out of slavery, past deep waters and through dry deserts into freedom. The celebration of Christmas honors not only a birth many centuries ago, but also the eternal descent of the divine Light into the depths of matter and the hearts of women and men today, symbolized by the burning of Christmas lights at the darkest season of the year and the sweet mystery of midnight on Christmas Eve.

The ethos of inner high adventure and kingly splendor, so well reflected in the outer lights and shadows of the Arthurian tales as told by Sir Thomas Malory and others, resonates with the spirit of this Path. Rides past fair castles in strange countries; rich, joyful revels at Camelot at which all were guests held in honor; King Arthur's custom never to eat at the high Feast of Pentecost until he had heard or seen some great adventure or marvel—all these wonders are parts of the seeker's inner treasure. From them stream the mysteries of faith that can hearten our own souls and thereby give joy to all whom we meet, friend and stranger alike.

On the basis of my own experience and that of others, I am endeavoring to interpret that intersection where the idea of the Path illuminates Christianity and Christianity illuminates the Path. What follows are essentially my own reflections. While no doubt substantially influenced by Theosophical teachers of esoteric Christianity such as Annie Besant, C.W. Leadbeater, and Geoffrey Hodson, this book does not rigorously follow them or anyone else, but rather, it presents my own views stemming from my own experience. It is not a work of systematic theology but more like a series of meditations on various aspects of esoteric Christian faith and life. Since Christianity today is divided into many schools and sects, I have also done all I can to make the present work truly ecumenical and interdenominational, in the hope that it will be of some help to Christians of any tradition who are prepared to see our common faith in the light of the great Path. Let blessings rest upon all.

1

WHAT WE ARE SEARCHING FOR

For some two millennia two images have haunted the spiritual dreams of the Christian West: the Cross and the Grail. The Cross is a symbol of suffering, yet it is also sometimes ornamented with gems. It suggests the outward face of Christianity, whether in the public agony of Jesus on Calvary or in the sign exalted on the steeples of countless churches. The Grail is a symbol of festive abundance, yet at the same time is hidden, seldom seen, not always thought of as outwardly splendid. It points toward the esoteric dimension of Christianity: to that which is hidden behind the outer form, is sought by knights who already wear the Cross, and is found only by the purest of the pure.

If the Grail represents the esoteric side of Christianity, its significance lies not only in its being found by just the few, but also in that it is found not by having the right answers, but by asking the right question. The reason Sir Galahad was able to see the Grail was because he correctly asked, "Whom does the Grail serve?"

Perhaps the same question could be asked of the esoteric Christianity that the Grail symbolizes: Whom, or what purpose, does esoteric religion serve?

There must be an inner side to a religion as old and widespread as that of Christianity. Does it matter if there is? Does it benefit the world in general, or anyone in particular? These are questions to ponder as you read this book.

Planet Earth is awash with religions and beliefs, and of those faiths, Christianity is the most prominent. About one-fourth of the Earth's people are Christian, at least in cultural background, and the faith remains vital. It has weakened now in its ancient stronghold of western Europe but is vigorous in the Americas and in newly-missionized areas of Africa and Asia. In the ex-communist countries, Christianity not only survives but can be credited for having exerted some degree of opposition to totalitarianism, in that it has represented the only aspect of life not completely controlled by the state. As usual, this picture is ambiguous; Christianity today, as in the past, is associated in some places with repugnant extremes of nationalism and anti-intellectualism. Yet it also gives expression to much that is positive, for example, the compassion of Mother Teresa and the advocacy for the poor in Latin America.

Indeed, Christianity is a religious world in itself, displaying a variety of forms as incredible as those of Hinduism: the colorful ritual of a Roman Catholic solemn high mass, the slow otherworldliness of the Eastern Orthodox liturgy, the deep silence of a Quaker meeting, the joyous babble of Pentecostal speaking in tongues, the dignified preaching of Presbyterianism, and much more.

Because of this ubiquity and influence, of all the religious images and thought-forms[1] of power floating in the world today, none are of more importance than those of Christianity. Some love it, some hate it, many are merely indifferent to it, finding the faith outmoded and irrelevant to their lives. And yet the Christian faith flourishes in many hearts. Indeed, it may be argued that in the dawn of the twenty-first century, after the fall of so many of the idols that once haunted the twentieth, from fascism and communism to excessive belief in human progress, Christianity may attain a new burst of vitality.

The problem with Christianity for some people is that it is not easily comprehensible on levels that mesh with the rest of their lives. Its Scriptures seem to speak of another world and another age in which miracles happened regularly and prescientific views of the universe were taken for granted. How do you make sense of a world of camels, shepherds, and kings in a life in which the dominant nonreligious images are far more likely to be of cars, corporations, and congresses? Some will say that our fundamental human problems remain the same, and no doubt they are right. But language and image are important for communication; some way must be found to comprehend the words that bridge the centuries.

Evangelicals and other conservatives within Christianity proclaim that the words of Scripture are above culture and must be taken on their own terms, judging and negating the culture when need be. Liberals, on the other hand, contend that faith must be correlated with the best scientific and philosophical

thought of each age and interpreted in terms sufficient to make it contemporary.

The esoteric approach of this book is somewhat
different from either of these positions. It does not
take the words of the faith—its biblical stories and
its doctrines—to be necessarily true in a historical or
scientific sense. Neither does it reduce them simply
to whatever comports with the current secular scientific worldview, as though infallibility had moved from
the Vatican to the laboratory and the university.
Rather, this perspective takes the stories and doctrines to be archetypes and thought-forms that have
a life and truth of their own, both because they are
believed and because they correspond to universal
truths—the "ancient wisdom"—known to profound
mystics and sages of all times and embedded in some
form in all the great religions. But these truths are
inward rather than literal—manifesting more in the
realms of the psyche than in the outer layers of the
universe.

Before developing this idea, however, let us again
consider Christianity as a contemporary world religion. The question naturally arises: if esoteric truth
can be found in all great religions, why should we
choose to work particularly with this one? There is
no absolutely compelling reason; on the other hand,
why not? Surely Christianity was founded by a great
Master and contains as fair a share of the ancient wisdom as do other religions; surely it lends itself as
soundly as any other faith to esoteric interpretation
and spirituality of practice. For one-fourth of the
world's population, it is the most familiar religion.

Further, Christianity can claim several unique and positive features in its teaching and historical role, from its affirmation of God's action and self-revelation in the midst of history and ordinary human life, to its role in many of the Western world's social reforms. So why not work with it?

ROMANTICISM AND CHRISTIANITY

One interesting claim to explore is that of the nineteenth-century clergyman and literary critic Stopford Brooke, cited in the Preface, that "Christianity is the most romantic of all religions." Romanticism, a literary and spiritual movement that began in the late eighteenth century, held that truth is best known and creativity is best expressed not through mere reason or facticity, but through imagination, feeling, freedom of expression, and introspection. Imagination, used in the highest sense of the word as forming mental images imbued with pure and powerful emotions to set against the mysteries of cosmos and self, was a way of knowing the inwardness as well as the surfaces of things. Stories, above all those which stretched the imagination through their treatment of the distant and the past or by moments of intense feeling, were exercises for the mind as well as ways of knowing.

From its beginning, European Romanticism had a special affinity for the Middle Ages, as reflected in the novels of Sir Walter Scott and many other Gothic writers. Romanticism was the key to the revival of interest in King Arthur, Camelot, and the Holy Grail, so well captured in Lord Tennyson's *Idylls of the King* and Richard Wagner's *Parsifal.* In all such works, themes of the quest come through powerfully like a distant but persistent melody: themes of a summoning and engaging sense of wonder, of conflict and suffering that is not just wasted energy but profoundly meaningful. In the end, tragedy fades into visions of glory shining down castle walls or manifesting in the unimaginable treasure of the Grail, a glory keener than any sorrow and inducing joy greater than anything the material world alone can give.

In all these respects, Christianity is indeed very romantic. Here, in the life of its greatest hero, Jesus Christ, is the quest embodied. In his words and parables and disturbing presence, the magical feel of something more—the kingdom of heaven—lies shimmering just beyond ordinary sight, like glimpses of gold caught out of the corner of one's eye. His sector of the Path led him to death on the Cross and, beyond all hope, to resurrection—the extremes of desolation and unexpected joy. His was a life on all the edges, cutting to the core of both the greatest darkness and the most brilliant light of which human life is capable, ending in joy which could only be contained by bringing in heaven, too. It was a life rich with a quality of meaning and fulfillment to which most of us can only aspire.

Here, then, in the life of Christ are all the essential elements of the hero myth: his remarkable birth, his ordeal, his triumph, and his return home. Here is the Divine Father and the Great Mother (in Mary) and the dying/rising god. Here also is the romance of association with times and places that are the stuff of legend in our cultural tradition, from Byzantium to Camelot. The story of Christ presents images that help us to link our inner universes with the outer cosmos and interpret our human significance in terms of the Whole. Though we may not die on a Cross or return to life in this world after death, we do know suffering, and we live all our days in the shadow of death. To understand the correlation between our suffering and our ultimate fulfillment is faith. Faith is not merely a way of knowing; it is also a way of participating.

On a somewhat more mundane level, note that just as romantics were much concerned with human relations, whether in terms of eternal love between two persons or of the ideal structure of society, so Christianity also is profoundly concerned with love on all levels and with the nature of communities. It views the church ideally as a community of love which affirms and supports all persons within it. While often the reality falls far short of the ideal, churches continue to try. Today perhaps more than ever, amid these dark and mazelike times, people come to the church as much, if not more, for community, for ordinary everyday support in family and personal life, as for the sake of more recondite doctrines or experiences. Yet Christian community has an esoteric meaning of its own.

But we are getting ahead of ourselves, giving answers before we ask the correct questions. What *are* we looking for in these gray years, when so much hope is gone and so many visions are punctured? Do possible vehicles for hope and vision remain? How do we begin to find them in our current cultural quagmire?

We can start, I believe, by asking ourselves and our world, so silent about the really important things, for some way to look up and see the stars turning in their great arcs, making years and cycles that extend almost to infinity. For in the last analysis, what we want is a sense that our lives, like Christ's, have some kind of long-term significance—not only for others, but also for ourselves. We want to be in touch with a level of reality beyond ourselves—to gaze beyond the one-dimensional obscurity of the present and know ourselves, as Jesus knew himself, to be on a Path far longer and greater than the span of this one life. This is the great Path, the Path through unimaginable worlds and ages on several planes that we have been following since we left our ultimate home. Those worlds are largely forgotten, but they have left traces in dreams and resonances that whisper almost without words deep within us. This Path will eventually take us Home again, and the whispers will turn to music.

On this journey, we would like to locate a community of seekers like ourselves with whom to share the travel. We yearn for the guiding wisdom of people who are in but not entirely of the present and who are here to do two things: survive with their souls intact and do all they can to help. We would like to be part of a brilliant and inspiring fellowship like that of the knights of the Round Table or the companions on the Grail quest, committed to sublime chivalric values and seeking together realities on the frontiers of human vision. Or we would like to be as those in the church's many orders and communities of faith, blessed with humility and living for service and not for themselves alone. We would like a community that is not only seeking and doing, but also has answers, however humbly expressed, and above all is committed to sharing love and support with us and our families. In these days of divorce, single-parenting, and the virtual demise of the old-fashioned extended family—stifling and yet so reliable and supportive—we yearn for anything that can even partly take the place of what we have lost. One reason religion remains alive in America today is because it offers virtually the only institutions that can begin to take the place of the extended family. We are looking for communities of faith that take the role of the family seriously.

Yet we also yearn for something that will caress our hearts as we wander through the modern spiritual wasteland: a practice—prayer, meditation, chant, ritual—able to lift us out of the flat plane of the present into a deeper, richer kind of consciousness, rooted in the fullness of the past and the wider circles of the universe. We want the rhythm of ritual, which has a different vibration from that of the mundane world around us.

Finally, for our minds as well as our hearts, we wish for a teaching and a worldview that unites self, community, practice, and universe into a meaningful whole—one that shows us why the world is as it is and then points us upward toward the moon and stars.

Above all, we desire to know that we are on the Path in the fullest sense of the word. We want to walk in a way that combines all three of the above: community, practice, and teaching. We inwardly crave a way that comes from somewhere and is going somewhere. We would like to be able to say as confidently as the Jesus of St. John's Gospel, "I proceeded and came forth from God; I came not of my own accord, but he sent me" (John 8:42). We seldom have this confidence, yet there is that in us which wants to ask: Where is the Father, the parent from which you came and I came? (John 8:18).

There is something within me which yearns to know that I have come from somewhere and am going somewhere, on more than just the biological level. I am a unique constellation of ideas, impulses, and dreams, yet I sometimes find it hard to interpret this ephemeral sense of self even to those nearest and dearest. Somewhere within me is a place known only to myself. It spreads before my inner eyes bright under the sun, a landscape strewn with star-fields of my favorite flowers. Beneath them are caverns even I have only partially explored, my trembling hands holding a torch that casts shadows greater than its light. But out of these fields and caverns come much of what I am and do, including those things that others—and sometimes even I—find hard to understand. Is there a Path to walk inwardly as well as outwardly? There is, and it can be expressed through esoteric Christianity.

This is not to say that Christianity, as it is now

outwardly expressed, is a perfect religion. All historically conditioned religions are limited by place, time, and culture. They all have learned much, but have much more to learn, before the end. Perhaps the time will come when each of them, including Christianity, will be superseded, their task in history complete. In my own view, Christianity needs to express more profoundly the interrelatedness of life and the full meaning of universal compassion, especially as those virtues are practically expressed in harmlessness and vegetarianism. Further, Christianity needs to relinquish its false spirit of exclusivity and the urge to judge the faith of others. It should refrain from confusing the right expression of faith with the expression of faith in the right words.

Yet on the level of esoteric Christianity, many of these shortcomings can be corrected. The romantic forms of the faith remain wondrous and capable of being comprehended on several planes. Esotericism always points beyond its visible symbols, knowing that none of them fully contain all truth but can only allude to it. It is therefore right to encourage those drawn to Christianity to remain with it, learn it from the inside out, and let it be a vehicle for esoteric understanding. The potential for this kind of learning and experience to occur exists in Christianity as completely as in any other faith.

The Nature of the Path

This world is made up of the drama of human life and human history. Behind it is the evolution of souls; behind these, the experience of the One; and behind all these, joy, *ananda*, bliss, peace, which is the true state of the One: hard to penetrate, hard to know by those of us still on the Path, yet nonetheless accessible.

The principle of this Path is to intuit—even to know—that our personal inner geometry of stars and shadows was formed over eons of experience on many worlds and is a legacy we must treasure until we finally arrive Home on the day all hearts share their secrets. At that time, all love will be consummated amid the unutterable wonder of knowing all others as we are known. All pilgrimages will come to rest, and all gathered riches will be enhanced a thousandfold through sharing in the giving and receiving of the final feast. And for each traveler, the end will come in its own time, for the Path is neither long nor short by human reckoning.

While the Path transcends our present single life, it clearly must also run through it—from birth to death, linking all the segments of this existence into a golden chain of deepening glow. Journeying through many climes, despite all hardships, to a spiritual goal is called a pilgrimage. The view of Theosophy is that the pilgrimage of a single life is a link in the chain of a far vaster pilgrimage, the odyssey from before the beginning to the final return to the Halls of Light.[2]

All that happens to us is of significance for this Path, though of course not all is helpful to our pilgrimage on it—some choices may set us back, others carry us forward. Sometimes we may need to progress with running leaps, sometimes with the steps of a stately dance. And, happily, we may find the company of fellow travelers along the way. Knowing we are on the Path accompanied by like-minded companions, we can ably push through the direst swamps with an eye on the trail markers and a communal song in the heart.

The Path is always there. Sometimes we may walk it well, with the help of a form of spirituality we know is right for us—a spirituality fitting so well that our real self is expressed and we know who we are deep within. We know no other spiritual path could be so right for us.

A spiritual way, with its practices, mind-set, and companions, is like a scenario for the real self. It is what you do with your inwardness that makes you feel most like your true self. In the midst of its work, you can say to yourself, "I am somebody." You are not just another face on the street, another hand in the factory or field, another presence moving uncertainly between family, friends, and job. You are that unique someone you know yourself to be deep down amidst the inner stars; and, with your spiritual practice, you are giving that unique self room to breathe. This is the pilgrim walking the Path from before time toward the final sharing and reunion.

When the way is alive and you are often embracing your real self, you are moving well on the Path. But all Pathwalking can and will at other times seem hard, discouraging, unreal—a mockery of what the walk ought to be. If this feeling persists, then certainly you need to take account of it and, without giving in to passing moods, carefully decide whether you need to look for a spiritual way better suited to you.

Sometimes the spiritual problem is in your own choices. Usually when you have made wrong choices not in accord with your real self, you know it. You say to yourself, "This is not me"; "I can't be doing this"; or "This can't be happening to me." Insofar as the hardship in question has been a result of your choice (which is not, of course, always the case), you know you have gotten off the Path and need to get back on it.

At other times it almost seems as though the Path is carrying *us*. Almost in spite of ourselves, we grow, we learn more about ourselves, and we catch glimpses of the gold at the end of life's rainbow just by living, even if we have consciously forgotten the pilgrimage. This may especially be true during the great events and crises of life: love, marriage, childbirth, work, sickness, even the passageway of death. In these hours our conscious minds are unable to focus clearly or fully on the Path, yet great changes are happening that will profoundly affect the inner and outer architecture of our lives.

We must let these occasions just occur, if they are in harmony with our real self, and ponder them in our hearts, even as the Blessed Mary did upon an angel's visit. Then, as soon as we can gain a perspective, we must consider the event in terms of the Path, asking: What have I learned? How have I grown? What new riches have I gained to carry Home? How has this experience deepened the mystery of life for me?

You know you are on the right track spiritually when the Pathworking seems to resonate with your inmost and truest self, the self you are when you are alone as well as with others, the self of your dreams and visions, the self of your subtlest joys. This book is for those for whom a Christian spiritual path seems right at that deep level. It is for those for whom the images of the Cross and Christ, the stories of the Bible, the devotional words of the Lord's Prayer and perhaps the Hail Mary, and the resonance of Protestant hymns or the drama of the Catholic liturgy have found a home in the secret places of the heart and are gateways to heavens within.

There are many paths within the Path. There are different religions and different ways of being Christian—Protestant, Catholic, Eastern Orthodox; liberal, evangelical; liturgical, free form—and of these various ways, one may seem right, the others less so, for each individual. From the perspective of Pathwalking, one could travel in this life over several alternative roadways. All this is a mystery. Only in the end will the reason for these varied experiences of the Path be fully known.

Understanding Esoteric Christianity

In esoteric Christianity, what is hidden behind the Cross and the Grail? What does *esoteric* mean? It means "hidden" or "concealed." An esoteric teaching is one that is not widely known but is concealed, perhaps in a private place or inside the wrapping of some other truth or apparent truth.

Truths may be hidden esoterically for several reasons. Sometimes they may be kept, like trade secrets, within a small circle of priests or practitioners for the sake of the power and privilege they bestow. Sometimes they are kept hidden out of the fear that, like the secrets of making atomic weaponry, the great power they contain would be highly dangerous in wrong or unknowing hands. It is thought in some circles that certain spiritual practices exist capable of generating forces that, if unwisely used, could release a Pandora's box of evils into the world comparable to those wrought by nuclear bombs in the hands of idiots. Just as some people are obviously more intelligent than others or more gifted in various areas of endeavor, some may be much more advanced in spirituality and in the ability to rightly understand and use spiritual things. Hence custodians of knowledge may argue that, even as sharp knives are kept out of the hands of small children, certain truths should be kept from those whose spiritual minds are still young.

Is this right? Why should any truths important to human spiritual growth, human welfare, even human sanity, be concealed and require initiation to be known? Why not leave them in the open, like stacks of silver coins in the public square, and let whoever wants to make use of them? Can't truth be its own guardian? The notion of withholding truth goes against our contemporary ideas of democracy and equal access.

Yet the reasons for withholding truth are good,

even necessary—not for the sake of a self-appointed elite, but for the sake of those who are not yet prepared to receive it. Truth must not be conveyed until the potential recipient is ready, just as a good teacher does not teach calculus before the student has learned counting. Some truths can only be rightly understood by someone who is prepared for them by initiation; until then, they must be sufficiently concealed to make such practice meaningful. Why are some people not born with the ability to receive the deeper truths? Unfortunately, it is evidently the nature of this world that they are not. That is an issue larger than esotericism. If most people were on the esoteric level of spirituality, there would be far less cruelty, war, and suffering than there is. Indeed, many wars are fought and much suffering is imposed out of allegiance to *exoteric* forms of religion—that is, the outer husks of forms and institutions. These exoteric forms can become identified all too easily with national loyalties and drives for power.

Whether or not this situation is as it should be, it is clearly the way things are in our present imperfect world. We must accept the reality of inequality, which in the end is the consequence of our own unwise choices, and allow the spiritually advanced to use their gifts in their own way for the benefit of all. Someday the rest of us will catch up.

Finally, truths may be esoteric simply because, while perhaps not even kept particularly concealed, they are understandable only to those who have reached a requisite level of training. Textbooks on calculus sit on library or bookstore shelves, but they are intellectually accessible only to those who have received the necessary preliminary training in arithmetic and algebra. In the same way, an esoteric legend may be in plain sight, but it is visible only to those with the ability to crack its code by seeing in it what others do not. Not a few signposts along the Path are of this sort. They are not hidden; yet they are grasped only by those who have the wisdom to read their language. To others wandering along the way, they may appear just as old stumps or barren rocks; no signposts are visible at all.

But learning to read the language and crack the code is an open secret, too. This is not an arcane tongue taught only in a few graduate schools. It is rather a language taught by experiences that shape not only our minds, but also our emotions and even our bodies, so that we are prepared to receive a new way of understanding life and of being in the world through all the levels of existence simultaneously. The language requires, in short, initiation.

ESOTERIC INITIATION

An initiation may be defined as an experience that imparts new knowledge or insight in the context of a total emotional and physical adventure powerful enough to inscribe the learning indelibly in one's consciousness. We have heard of the overwhelming, sometimes horrendous, initiations administered in some tribal societies, with terror, deprivation, bodily mutilation, instruction in tribal lore, and possibly meeting one's patronal spirit on a vision quest all as parts of the ordeal. We also know of the only somewhat more benign initiations in college fraternities, and their equivalents for novices in a strict monastery or for new recruits at army boot camp. And we may be aware of the dramatic initiations conducted by various spiritual orders. In every case, it is clear that more than just teaching is involved; it is teaching in a context that makes the experience unforgettable, that engraves its emotional power on the heart and bonds one with others sharing the same teaching.

All initiations actually fall back on the greatest symbol of all: spiritually dying and coming back to life. They all center on a passage that means dying to one kind of life—the life of the child or the outsider to a group—and being reborn into another: as the adult or a member of the order. Sometimes the death and rebirth imagery is very graphic, as in Christian baptism by immersion: sinking deep into the cleansing waters of death and the womb, and then arising out of them spiritually as a new person.

Actually, initiations may be of several kinds. "Programmatic" initiations such as those just cited may be arranged and undertaken voluntarily or by select groups. Yet there are also what may be called "natural" initiations. We all go through these just by living: birth, puberty and adolescence, education, marriage, childbearing, sickness, death. Each of these entails dying to one kind of life and being reborn into another: child into adult, single person into spouse, childless woman into mother. All such major transitions can and do involve initiatory ordeals and tremendous emotional experiences as forceful as any contrived by a programmed initiation. Societies often mark these personal transitions with public ceremonies: confirmations and other religious rites of puberty, graduations, weddings, funerals. Thus an individual event becomes part of something programmatic for the whole social order as well. Finally, in addition to such natural and programmatic initiations, Theosophists and others talk about initiations received in dreams, in out-of-the-body experiences, and in near-death experiences.

Whatever the variety, some kind of initiatory experience is necessary in order to rightly grasp esoteric truth. Just as a child may wonder about adulthood, badger her parents with questions about it, and dress up like an adult, she will not *really* know what adulthood is like until she has passed through puberty and adolescence and arrived there; nor will she *really* know what marriage is like until the wedding bells have rung . . . and the honeymoon is over.

Our position, and that of Theosophy in general, is that much of the spiritual truth in the world is esoteric truth that will resist being fully grasped until the seeker has gone through an initiation—be it programmatic, natural, or dream—appropriate to the kind of truth it is. Further, our position is that much of Christian truth, in its full innermost meaning regarding the Path and the long pilgrimage, is of this nature.

We must not undertake esoteric learning and initiation with a sense of pride that they will make us intrinsically superior to other human beings. We study esotericism and receive initiations not to be better than others, but only to be better than our own former selves; and this determination comes out of deep humility, realizing how poor we are in the things of the spirit. Pride is recognized as the greatest sin of all, the prime and original sin of Satan, in conventional Christian tradition. It is also the greatest sin in esotericism, though in a slightly different sense, where it refers above all to the egotistical sense of self-sufficiency of the person who believes she or he can do without God or divine grace. It relates to an egotistical sense that one is now privy to secret knowledge, and that although a "god in the making," one is godlike already, with special powers and even special moral values. There have been those esotericists who were tempted by the dark side of the Path and wanted to use what they thought they had learned as a means to power rather than love. But in this world, even the lures of dark spirituality are likely to be delusions, for few indeed are truly able to employ the esotericism of hell any better than most are that of heaven. However, the wonderful thing about the esotericism of heaven as opposed to hell is that, to begin its attainment, you don't need to be of diabolical intelligence. You need only to be willing to humble yourself and acknowledge your present hollowness and need. As the Sermon on the Mount tells us, the blessed are none other than the poor in spirit, those who mourn, the meek, those who hunger and thirst after righteousness, the merciful, the pure in heart, the peacemakers, and the persecuted (Matt. 5:1-11). If nothing else, we can empty ourselves of all pride until we meet these criteria.

Clearly, the particular world in which we now live looks as if it were designed for souls going through one of the dark passageways of the Path. It seems the great majority who pass this way are required to become spiritually poor and find the Path anew, if they are able, through a quest and a defining initiatory ordeal; then they are to carry the treasure of that experience on with them. This situation cannot be blamed on karma or unconscionable fate. We set up the conditions of this world ourselves, largely by making life choices that blind us to more than the surface of things, to which our attention is limited; and we likewise blind our children, who will only with difficulty know more than what they see in us.

At the same time, the reality of inner universal esoteric truth makes the situation more democratic than it might be otherwise, for the real truth resides within all faiths and so is accessible to anyone of any culture. The esoteric principle makes finding hidden truth a quest, requiring commitment, growth, and salutary experience. As in any treasure hunt, you have to keep at it and learn to see tracks, shifts in the wind, and the corner sticking out of something almost entirely hidden from view.

This treasure of spiritual truth is not going to be where we first expect it, and so we need not look for it only in our home faith. But it is not necessarily going to be found where we *least* expect it, either. We need not seek it *only* in temples banked with Himalayan snow. Truth is neither near nor far. Indeed, the profoundest truth is found above all in the temple of our own hearts, but few can see into it until the mirror of religion has been held up to them. The way Home can be strewn with unexpected clues we learn to peruse, and this can be a lesson as well, for there are many clues we too casually overlook: clues of wisdom, of fortune and future, and of love.

Finally—and this is particularly important with regard to understanding Christianity—the esoteric truth hidden within a religion allows those who are still prepared to worship only in its external forms to also have a spiritual life of great value. For these people are also facing, so to speak, in the right direction, unknowingly but significantly honoring the principle behind the image: the transcendent Christ behind the Cross as well as the crucified Jesus. Through the exercise of love and devotion, they are training themselves to transcend lower aspects of the self, which is not only good in itself but is also a preparation for later initiations.

However, great dangers lurk on this part of the Path. It is all too easy to absolutize the preliminaries and the outward forms; to make an idol out of the material or mental image; or even to castigate or kill those subscribing to another outward, verbal, or mental form. Yet pure devotion can create thought-forms that channel grace from the heart of reality and open inner windows of receptivity toward it. Take, for example, the thought-form of the Cross.

Esoteric Christian Symbology

The Cross is a symbol that has inspired passion throughout history, from the slaughter wrought by the hacking swords of crusader knights to the tenderest devotion of St. Francis. It is also a symbol with great inherent meaning. Historically, it is the instrument of the death of Jesus, the Christ or Messiah, and it also represents the religion given his name. As such, the Cross is mounted on Christian altars, atop cathedrals, and on the crowns of kings and queens who claimed to rule in Jesus' name.

The Cross also has a sequence of inward meanings. For those who see inwardly, it is a sign both of suffering and of hope. On the one hand, it weeps for Christ's excruciating suffering in this hard world, which did not exempt even him who is called the "king of kings"; on the other, it sings of hope brighter than the blackest Calvary and joy keener than the sharpest pain. For the lore tells us that Christ was seen again, and to symbolize faith in his resurrection, crosses on the altars of Christendom are often studded with gems that serve as peepholes to the glory behind pain and death.

Finally, the Cross has a universal, nonhistorical meaning. Its four directional arms signify the cosmos itself, the eons-old world of physical form; and the breaking of Jesus' heart and wholeness upon the Cross conveys that all of us who bear the fire of soul within are crucified upon the Cross of matter. How often we yearn for beauties and adventures beyond the limits of our frail flesh and dream of life beyond that confined between womb and tomb!

Yet there is hope, indeed, for death happens *in* time, but eternity *transcends* time. Matter is not just the hard Cross; it is also the pliant life-giving flesh of the eternal Mother, who in this drama is Mary, Mother of Jesus, while Jesus himself is the eternal Word or patterning form of God's creation. Together, living form and living matter, they bring forth the universe with its shoals of stars.

It is important to realize that in this drama the two, imaged as male and female, child and mother, pattern and matter, are equally creative and eternal. The female is not merely the passive instrument of the male, just as the eternal Word is not merely the child of the eternal Mother. The Mother, although she is matter with form, is also Sophia, meaning *Wisdom*—the feminine principle of wisdom and the wisdom of the universe itself embedded in its very substance; the knowing consciousness of the atom that plays its own role in the making of the universe as we know it, shaping with female brilliance its lineaments and its delights. In the Scriptures, the Mother tells us that "When he marked out the foundations of the earth, then I was beside him, like a master worker; and I was daily his delight, rejoicing before him always" (Prov. 8:29-30). Her role in creation clearly continues to be active: "Wisdom cries aloud in the street; in the markets she raises her voice; on the top of the walls she cries out; at the entrance of the city gates she speaks" (Prov. 1:20-21). She is also the Lady of the Feast: "Wisdom has built her house, she has set up her seven pillars . . . she has also set her table. She has sent out her maids to call from the highest places in the town" (Prov. 9:1-3).

The pain and joy of the creative process is shared between ageless Mother and Son, with all the wonder and delight that a mother and child can know looking into each other's eyes. The inevitable confining of spirit to the structures of matter is necessary for the sake of individualization and expression. The eternal story of creation and confinement is enacted in historical time—for the benefit of us who live in this world—in the drama of Jesus' birth, death on the Cross of matter, and resurrection. All human experience in this world *must* be set into the frame of time and history—yet, like a golden sky behind it, there is a reality beyond time as we know it.

This is what is meant by esoteric truth in Christianity: It really is, for us, about the sky behind time and the Path winding up into it. For although esotericism may tell us eternal truths, these truths are most real for us when they involve *our* walking the Path here and now in space and time. They also reveal where the Path originated from and where it is going. The truth of the eternal Mother of God and the eternal Word of God shows us that on the Path in a universe such as this one, crosses and resurrections will occur; and they will be invitations to wisdom's feast and opportunities for glances of glory further down the way. And in future ages, the same drama may be played again, though with different actors.

Christian esoteric truth shows us that the Christian path we may follow in this particular life is part

of that great Path through the worlds back to the ultimate Home. This means, of course, that any stories and doctrines making the faith of Christ a narrow, exclusive religion, with its eyes on one life and
one death only, must be given wider, esoteric meaning. We can hear this meaning in the explanations
Jesus himself saved for those disciples he regarded
as ready for them: "Unto you is given to know the
mystery of the kingdom of God: but unto them that
are without, all these things are done in parables"
(Mark 4:11).

The Path is indeed the kingdom of God, and
the kingdom of God is indeed the Path, as it is also
the goal. Both are realities greater, richer, and deeper
in space and time than our world; they are *in* our world
yet not *of* it. Both can be seen in clues and parables
by those who are sensitized: for example, look at the
parables of the mustard seed; the lost coin and the
widow's offering; the feast for the returned prodigal
son; and the similar feast for all on the day of light.
The Path and the kingdom are of far greater worth
than all the glories and temptations of this world, all
of which may well be divested for their sake. The
Path is the pearl of great price. With work, it will
best be understood by those with the sanctified simplicity and singleness of mind of a wise child. "Let
the children come to me, and do not hinder them,
for of such belongs the kingdom of heaven" (Matt.
19:14).

The Symbols of Cross and Grail

The relation of the Cross and the Grail is an interesting one: the dirt, sweat, and blood of real history against the romantic dreamworld of the heart. The Cross meant death of a particularly cruel, degrading, and lingering sort favored by the Romans for unruly slaves and rebels of low status. The Grail, by contrast, sings of heraldry, festive halls, and heroic quests by knights of the purest blood. The Cross represents Christianity's outward sufferings in a grim world, the Grail its silvery inward glories.

Yet the complete story is not so simple. Over the years the rugged Cross, as previously mentioned, has come to be washed in gold, set with precious stones, and placed between candlesticks on altars of marble. The Grail has a legendary role as the cup Jesus held up before his disciples in that plain upper room as he said, "This is my Blood of the New Covenant," and as the cup which received the blood from his pierced veins in the darkness of the next afternoon. Despite the romance around it, the Grail has been visualized as a utilitarian chalice of unremarkable simplicity, distinguished only by a supernatural glow from deep within, perceptible to those with unclouded eyes.

Nor is their symbolic destiny simple. The Cross, as mysterious as the kingdom of God both in and out of this world, has meant both kingship and suffering, and beyond that the strange regal power exercised on the inner planes by those of the meek who suffer well, in love. It is often called the answer to the world's woes, and its message is preached to the nations. The Grail, on the other hand, was glimpsed only at the end of a great quest by the boldest and most select of knights—and its power was unlocked not by an answer, but by asking the right question: "What is the Grail and whom does it serve?" No sounds, words, or thoughts in any language then or now could frame the answer to this question. Much less could any deed of arms win the secret of the Grail.

It was enough that the question be truly asked for life to be restored to the wasteland and for a knight such as Galahad to find true and undying honor, his face shining with the glory of the oft-hidden Grail as he gazed into its luminous depths. Then, his mission accomplished, that purest of knights continued on the Path and passed altogether beyond the circles of this world.

The Grail Legend

The Grail, like the Kingdom of God and the Cross behind the cross, serves as the emblem for the esoteric heart of Christianity. The Grail narrative has several overlapping versions. What follows is an account of the story that seems to best present the Grail's spiritual significance:

Word reached the court of King Arthur at Camelot that somewhere in Britain a land was wasting away under a baleful enchantment, because Pellam, the king of that country, was wounded, and a magical object in his keeping had been desecrated.

There was nothing astounding about this in itself. All through the ancient world, land and sacred king lived in deep communion, so that the health of one affected the health of the other. When the king, who was high priest as well as ruler to his people, became unworthy or unfit, heaven blighted his kingdom with famine and loss of fertility. But the case of Pellam was especially grievous, for it was rumored that the sacred object was none other than the chalice which Christ had used at the Last Supper and which the next day had caught his precious blood.

Joseph of Arimathea, who had arranged for the Savior's burial, had then brought the sacred cup to England, building a castle to shelter it as well as the spear that had pierced the dying Lord's side. The care of the two priceless relics had been entrusted to Joseph's descendants down the years, and King Pellam was the present guardian.

But now, something had gone seriously wrong. Some said the disaster was due to the earlier unknowing incursion into the Grail palace by a knight of Camelot called Balin. He had disrupted its peace with fighting and then, intruding clumsily into the Holy of Holies, he had panicked at the place's air of supernatural mystery and struck King Pellam in the groin with the relic spear. Upon the monarch's being maimed, the land had grown barren. Balin was told that only the right word would save the king and his land, but to speak it was beyond the ability of a rough warrior such as he.

Hearing of the tragedy, knights began trying to find their way through the wasteland to the sanctuary of the Grail. That was no easy task, for the place was not entirely of this world. Sometimes the castle was visible; sometimes a quester would see only dust and withered trees. Some would come upon a lake with a mysterious fisherman who might give enigmatic directions and who was actually the wounded king. It was clear that the entire adventure involved entering a realm more akin to dream and myth and the ultimate roots of consciousness than to solid earth. Yet King Pellam's realm and the sanctuary of the Grail were nonetheless real, overwhelmingly real, for those with eyes to see them.

The first to arrive was Lancelot, the greatest knight in the world, yet flawed by untoward desire for Arthur's wife, Queen Guinevere. He found the castle and saw its splendor and the pitiful king lying on his pallet. As Lancelot waited in the great hall, he witnessed a strange procession. Maidens bore past him food and drink, and then a young man upheld a spear dripping blood from its tip; finally, a young woman of fabulous beauty carried an object, draped in white cloth, from which glowed uncanny light. But much as he desired to see what was beneath that coverlet, Lancelot was not permitted to do so. By an enchantment, however, he did spend that night with the Grail maiden, who was King Pellam's daughter, and of that union was born a son.

That child became the knight Sir Galahad, who years later made his appearance at King Arthur's court. At that time, knights were still setting off in quest for the Grail. Percival was one of them—a knight sincere to the point of naiveté, always a bit too gullible and literal, yet of unquestioned bravery and faithfulness. He indeed reached the Grail castle and saw the procession of the bleeding spear and the covered holy object. But when Percival opened his mouth to speak, no words came. He was coldly led to his bedroom, and when he awoke, the sacred courts were empty and ruined. He had failed. Many other knights did not even reach the castle.

But then came Galahad, the knight of surpassing beauty and purity, grandson of King Pellam and son of the world's finest knight, who had been begotten and born for this very hour. He had sat once in the Siege Perilous—the seat at Arthur's round table reserved for the greatest of all—which even his father Lancelot had refused because of the one stain on his honor. While the young Galahad had sat in that chair, the Grail had appeared for a moment, seeming to glow and shimmer in the air above the famous table, as though in prophecy that it would be Galahad himself who would accomplish the highest of all deeds: succeeding at the Grail quest.

Now Galahad arrived at the Grail castle, accompanied by Sir Bors and the returning Sir Percival. The three splendid knights all saw the procession—the offerings, the youth with the crimsoned spear, the maiden bearing the precious chalice. But only Galahad spoke. From deep within him, out of his destiny and his purity of heart, came the words clearly:

What is the Grail and whom does it serve?

At that very moment, a bell echoed throughout the ancient structure, and then came the song of birds and the rustle of rain as spring returned to the barren wasteland. King Pellam arose, healed, full of his former youth and vigor. Galahad was shown the Grail unveiled and looked far into its depths, his face radiant with mystic rapture and sublime wisdom beyond words. He then slumped into graceful death, his task done, ready to sail on his inner voyage to other and better worlds.

This is the story of the esoteric Grail legend. The Cross, though it has its esoteric meanings, also represents the exoteric or *outer* meaning of Christianity: the death of a particular man at a particular historical moment who, in the words of the Creed, "suffered under Pontius Pilate, was crucified, died, and was buried." It is the main public symbol of the faith, appearing on churches and altars, book covers, and even the jewelry of the faithful. But the Grail is an almost entirely *inward* symbol, known only to a relative few, visible to fewer still, fulfilled not in answers but in a question and a realization beyond words, beyond space and time, between this world and the next.

Both are important. Both must radiate their light. And here we shall endeavor to see how the increasingly esoteric answers behind the Cross can lead to the question and the light of the Grail.

2

THE HOLY TRINITY: CHRISTIAN MEANING IN THE THREE OUTPOURINGS OF CREATION

CONSCIOUSNESS AND MATERIALISM

re you conscious? Can you prove it? For that matter, is anyone else conscious and can that be proven? Or are we all just automatons, programmed to walk around acting as though we were conscious? Could you be the only truly conscious being in the universe and all the rest of us be only seemingly conscious robots put here for your bane or benefit?

Ridiculous questions? Consider the implications. Looking at ourselves and everything else only from the point of view of our outward behavior, it may appear highly likely that you and I are *both* conscious. Indeed, it could be impossible to tell the difference between a conscious being and a perfectly computerized simulation of the same—at least until, as in the Grail story, the right question is asked: a question only a truly conscious being could correctly ask or answer. Without consciousness, we might just be the centerpieces of some ultra high-tech civilization from which sentient beings have long vanished but which continues to operate into eternity under the guidance of unknowing but sophisticated, self-repairing computers. Trains run on time, hospitals treat their mechanical patients, wars are fought—unconsciously, but who can say to what end?

You say, I know I am conscious. But can you take out your consciousness and show it to me? Can you even describe just what it is? If we start from the materialistic assumption that matter—molecules, atoms, subatomic particles—in its nonconscious guise is the basic reality of the universe, consciousness has no necessary or discernible place. Some cosmological and quantum physics models *do* posit consciousness as a necessary component of the existence of the universe; Theosophy, and in a real sense all religions, concur in this view. But let us consider the implications of the contrary view, the materialistic one. In it, consciousness is an orphan that somehow appeared on the doorstep of humanity—or maybe it is an illusion altogether. In any case, in the materialistic view it is not necessary to take consciousness into account to understand how the cosmos works—or even, at least according to behavioral psychology, to understand how human beings work. This minimalism can also be found in the basic applied sciences that operate for all intents and purposes *without* positing universal consciousness—even if the scientists themselves *are* conscious. This kind of science underpins the outer structures, and increasingly the mental structures, of the modern world: its industry, medicine, computers, space exploration, and psychology.

And it operates very well. I suspect that, for all our occasional grumbling about the dehumanization of science and technology, few of us are really prepared to return to the ox-carts and brief life-expectancy of the Middle Ages—plagues and serfdom can dehumanize, too. Nonetheless, we can't help feeling uneasy. Somehow, somewhere, something is being left out. How else to explain the persistence of religion and the growing interest in spiritual healing and everything "new age"? Of science itself we might ask the Grail question, "Whom does it serve?"

Some observers at the frontiers of the material sciences—especially physics and cosmology—tell us that in those disciplines, matter ultimately appears to fizzle out into something else . . . but what that something is, it is hard to say. It is becoming more and more evident that materialism is not about matter at all. It is about mathematics. No one knows what matter really is, or even if it exists. All we know is that mathematical models of how matter appears to work have enough predictive value to make the wheels of modern science and technology turn. Even so, those exploring the farthest frontiers are beginning to wonder if the ultimate universe may not be a lot different than the universe we now think we know.

Maybe the way we think of the universe is a partial view so restricted by our tiny range of perception that it amounts to a vast illusion. Our view may caricature the real universe, functioning just well enough to keep us limited to the pitiful puddle that is all we know of the galactic ocean. Perhaps we are like the inmates of Plato's cave, content with the shadows made by realities beyond their understanding. Or, using the mathematical model, perhaps we are like students working out a very complex problem: We are using the wrong formula, but it is nonetheless a formula that produces answers sufficiently within the "ballpark" of likelihood that we don't realize the mistake for some time. At length, other answers begin to come in—perhaps regarding why there is consciousness in the first place—that make us realize how serious the discrepancy is between our perceptions and the truth. Then, very reluctantly, we have to go back to the beginning of the problem and look for a new formula.

Of course, it is possible to go to the opposite extreme from materialism. Philosophical idealists past and present have contended that since consciousness is all that we know from within, it is fair to argue that consciousness is all that exists. The supposedly material world we see around us is simply constructed by our "categories of perceptions" (Immanuel Kant's term) out of who can say what raw materials—all we know or can know is how the world is put together in our minds. Or there is the dualism of René Descartes, who started with the consciousness-affirming postulate, *Cogito ergo sum*—"I think, therefore I am"—but who believed that consciousness existed at the controls of an unconscious, mechanical body in a materialistic world. This has been called the "ghost-in-the-machine" view. The trouble with Descarte's postulate is that it limits our concept of *being* to *thought*. This philosophy leads finally to what has always been the curse of Christianity and of several other religions, including some modern psychological, "new age" therapies: an excessive emphasis on soul-saving subjectivity, the attitude being to save the soul or "real self" and cast aside the material body as "container." These spiritualities are too one-sided if they locate the sacred in the mind alone and not also in the universe. In the esoteric or Theosophical view, consciousness and matter are *always* together and spring from the same source, like the proverbial two sides of the same coin. Yet they are not reducible one to the other, so as to make matter nothing but a projection of thought, or consciousness nothing but an excretion of matter at a particular level of organic complexity. Reality *is*, and is always, both subjective *and* objective, inner *and* outer. This can only be understood in the total context of the whole universal environment.

THE NATURE OF CONSCIOUSNESS

No doubt these positions on consciousness are as hard to prove or disprove as is flat-out materialism. But there *is* one test case, one pure sample, of the universe in all its baffling complexity that is accessible to each of us. With it we can each launch our own probe into inner space or begin a Grail quest for ultimate truth. That sample is— ourselves! Assuming that we ourselves are parts of the universe, that we came out of it and so reflect something of its inner and outer nature, we must assume that what we are is at least potentially present in everything, and vice versa. Let us therefore look deeply within ourselves.

This kind of reflection can truly be done only in the stillness of deep meditation. Here, all we can do is review the results many have found on that inward exploratory expedition. At the deepest level, they have reported a profound quiet consciousness that remains—calm, sparkling, joyous—even when the ordinary activity of mind is brought to cessation. Above this level arises the consciousness of things, whether figments of dream or fantasy or imagination, or perceptions in the mind of the real world. Next come the kinds of words and mental images that we use to solve problems, whether mechanical or personal or philosophical, or even just to talk to ourselves about things. After that come the emotions, which provide feelings to go with the thoughts: the whole gamut from joy to rage, fascination to fear, love to lethargy. Finally, there is awareness of the body, with all its permutations and subtle kinds of body feelings: tension and tiredness, hunger and thirst, pain and zest. And through the body—that is, through the five senses—comes awareness of the outside world.

Oddly, though, the world of which we have awareness is almost as much inside us as outside, for its products—and their images—dominate the inner life much of the time. We need food, drink, air, shelter, and so we think and fantasize about them a lot. Our consciousness requires as *its* food and drink manageable relations with that world, especially with other people. With them we exchange language, ideas, hopes, fears, passionate physical contacts, and traumatic struggles. We are part of all we meet, and it of us, on many levels. So our consciousness is connected with the body and the body with the world, and the network of connections extends out and out . . . into unknowable infinity.

And why should not all components of the universe, from starfish to stars, be similarly configured, with an inside and an outside, a consciousness and a body and everything in between, and interconnections that go on and on? Of course, regarding both the sunfish and the sun we may not see all the layers but only the surfaces; we must intuit the interior from the sample test case that is ourselves. This is what esotericism, including esoteric Christianity, is really all about: the inside as well as the outside—with inner stairwells running up and down from matter to consciousness—and the wisdom that becomes available in that kind of universe.

That wisdom has sometimes been called "secret" or "hidden," though it really is in plain sight if you look at things steadily and in the right way—maybe with the help of a meditation-born multi-dimensional mirror. It has sometimes been called the "ancient wisdom" because there were those in ancient times who knew it as well or better than anyone today, for it is not the kind of wisdom that depends on outward forms of progress. Indeed, this kind of wisdom may actually be lost in the glamour of "progress." Yet all that was known to the earliest sages is as available now as ever, if we look into the deep levels of light behind the eyes.

Esoteric wisdom concerning the inward/outward nature of humans and things is that the levels of reality indicated by this kind of perception don't stop at our skin. A fundamental assumption of esotericism, based on the test case—you or me—is that if it's anywhere, it's everywhere. For there is no reason to think that you or I are living freaks in a dead universe. It is far more reasonable to think that whatever we are is spread throughout the universe and pervades every atom therein.

Furthermore, esoteric wisdom presumes that the levels or kinds of consciousness have correspondences throughout the cosmos, too, or at least that their roots extend all the way through it. If in our sample probe we encounter an emotional and feeling realm, if we survey the mental realm and the ability to make thought-forms, if we find the stratum of intuitive awareness, and if deep down we touch the substratum of God-like, pure being-knowledge-joy consciousness, then these must also all exist throughout the galaxies, at least as potential manifestations. The esoteric wisdom tradition rejects as arbitrary and unwarranted by scientific or spiritual evidence any doctrine that considers humanity a special creation separate from the rest of the universe or from the full physical and spiritual evolution of Earth. We were not made on the spot or dropped into this universe that is now our home from some other sphere. Esotericism fully accepts the teaching behind the story in Genesis, which says that humanity was made from the dust of the earth and was infused with the same breath of the Holy Spirit that ruffled the waters of chaos on the first day.

Using words to explain the nature of conscious-ness and religious truths can be confusing. Some-times people want to reject the use of words and ideas in religion altogether, saying that nothing matters ex-cept good experiences and good feelings. But reli-gion needs an intellectual framework in addition to experience; otherwise, we are likely to become ex-periential junkies or spiritual tourists flitting from one sacred site or rite to another, whether outwardly or subjectively, without ever getting anywhere. The-osophy and its interpretation of esoteric Christianity can provide a framework on which we can build.

But clearly in this context words cannot be used in quite the same way as when we talk about the best way to drive to work or whether it will rain to-morrow. In speaking of things above the normal range of sensory experience, we are confronted with the reality of many kinds of truth or, more accurately, many languages for the one truth. At this point, we need humility before the power and the limitations of language, especially in the borderlands between the seen and the unseen and the human and the tran-scendent.

In these borderlands, the best that words can do is point toward the truth. But even when language is direct and effective, it is overwhelmingly clear that the word is not the same as the thing it refers to, anymore than a map or sign is the same as the loom-ing majestic mountain it indicates. Words like "God," "Logos," "Christ," "Holy Spirit," "outpouring," "atma," "soul," "mental/astral plane," and "demon/

unclean spirit" are poor pointers to reality, yet they must do.

THE NATURE OF MYTH

Myth—or to use in a word with slightly different connotations, *allegory*—has a special role in esoteric Christianity. In religious discourse, especially the esoteric, we use the word *myth* very differently from the common use of the word, which is basically to describe something that is not true. "Oh, that's just a myth," people say, dismissing whatever it is. If the meaning of *myth* as something false is the one that obtrudes on your mind, use *allegory* instead. But in esoteric Christianity, *myth* properly means a story that, while it may not be literally true, nevertheless embodies truth at the highest level. The truths of myth in this sense of the word are eternal and universal, but so great and so far beyond ordinary language that they fall flat if just stated as philosophical abstractions. They vividly come to life only if expressed in the form of an image or story. For example, most Christians would agree that when Scripture (Heb. 10:12) and the creeds speak of Jesus sitting at the right hand of God after his ascension into heaven, we are not to take this image literally, since God is everywhere. Rather, the image depicts the intimate relationship between God the Father and God the Son. The pictures of myth may not be factual, but that is not their point. Myths were never true but are always true.

But who is actually telling the story of a myth or

allegory? You and I don't just make up stories like those in the Bible ourselves; rather, *the stories are already there. The truths themselves tell the stories.*

These stories are not just fiction. They are written about real people and real events. They are written on the pages of days and in the books of years, in real time and real life—or life as real people saw it. When we read these stories with their overtones of transcendent reality, if we are attuned to esoteric experience we don't respond to them just because of the teller's status or because the book is supposed to have an external supernatural authority. We respond because we recognize deep within ourselves that these stories are written about *us*. We know that their truth was inscribed on our hearts before the written text gave them to us in words we can read. These myths come from the source of all great stories—eternity as it breaks into time, like waves of the infinite ocean crashing onto the shores of the world.

For Christians, the myths are the stories in the Bible—above all the stories of the life and death and resurrection of Jesus in the New Testament. These stories tell of timeless realities in a form that makes it seem as though they happened at specific times and places: in the case of the New Testament, some two thousand years ago in Palestine.

There is at least one exception to my statement that myths are never factual but always true: Christian myths lay claim to both historical *and* eternal truth. These stories are accounts of events that actually *did* happen at this or that time and place, *and* they are myths and allegories of the eternal. Not every detail may be factual as recorded, for scholars argue about them. But in broad outline, which is what matters in myth, the life of Christ was no doubt a reality, and the parts that may not be historical, such as his ascension and sitting at the right hand of God, have significant allegorical meaning. The search for the meaning of the myth is like the search for the Grail and whom it serves.

Nonetheless, for Christians Jesus is the main historical manifestation of the Christ, the universal divine creative principle immanent in the natural and human world, and the Christ is the main manifestation in creation of God. Certainly there have been other manifestations on earth—Confucius, Buddha, Muhammad—but as things have worked out in history, Jesus seems to have been a more universal manifestation for all of the earth, and the others more for particular cultures, at least from our current perspective. That role is born out of Jesus' life and death and what they represent on the spiritual plane. For unlike other manifestations of God, he did not really establish a traditional law or a particular spiritual or devotional practice. Rather, Jesus demonstrated spiritual power through the universal themes and experiences of suffering, unjust persecution, torture, death, and then the marvelous renewal of life. Therein lies the historical power of Christianity.

Christianity is exceptional among world religions in that it is based not just on words but on events that took place not in some inaccessible and undatable mythical realm, like the stories of Zeus or

Krishna, but in specific historical times. "In those days there went out a decree from Caesar Augustus . . . ," says the Gospel of Luke. "He suffered under Pontius Pilate," says the Nicene Creed. These specific occurrences in the harsh days of the Roman Empire can be dated and set beside other historical events. In other words, while Christianity is based on myths, they are myths that are largely grounded in real events, embodying things of the spirit in the blood, sweat, and grime of real time. The perception that these events are meaningful in terms of eternal realities is, of course, what we ourselves add. This perception is in part what is meant by faith.

MYTH AND CREATION

What meaning do these myths embody? Let us consider the story of creation as presented in Theosophy and the esoteric Christianity related to it. This model of creation is no doubt derived from Neoplatonism, which was so influential both in early Christian thought and in the Theosophical tradition. It says that the unknown God is revealed to the world *in* the world—just as the hidden Grail is revealed in the abundance that flows from it—and is active in the world, creating the cosmos out of preexistent but unformed matter. God, or the "Unknown Root," as Helena Blavatsky calls it, is beyond name and form and even myth. Nevertheless, God—as manifested in the world—is known mythically by three Greek terms that we recognize as the Holy Trinity: *ens*, the One, is God the Father; *logos*, the creative word, is

God the Son; and *psyche*, or soul, is God the Holy Spirit, the Lord and Giver of life.

Esoteric Christians since the author of St. John's Gospel have understood creation in terms of this Holy Trinity, believing that the three aspects of God brought about the world by interacting with the eternal sea of matter, the Mother. In mythic terms, the creation did not merely take place in the unfathomable past but is eternally recurring in us. For, of that Father and Mother we are born. We are children first of heaven, then of the stars, and then of the old, old oceans of the earth. Our bodies contain the salt of the sea, and our souls harbor stars and glimmerings of heaven. As without, so within. If we truly see the dawn and know it as the ancient ones did, all the oceans within will turn to light. For the true light that enlightens everyone (John 1:9) will then have been seen in its cosmic dimensions, even as it was seen by Jesus, in whom the dawn from above has broken upon us (Luke 1:78).

THE THREE OUTPOURINGS OF CREATION

Creation in this mystical perspective is a series of three Outpourings by the three principles of the Holy Trinity. According to the esoteric teaching, the first Outpouring is actually of the third person, God the Holy Spirit. Many Christians, especially those following esoteric Christianity, regard the Holy Spirit as feminine; archetypally, it seems to have both masculine and feminine qualities. The Book of Genesis tells us that in the beginning the Spirit of God moved over the face of the waters—the activity of God entering the inchoate sea of unformed primordial matter. The Hebrew word for "spirit" also means "wind," and one can imagine a dark, still and somber sea suddenly stirred to life as a fresh breeze sweeps across it, causing the waters to crest in bright, lively waves full of sound and foam—the rising and falling forms of creation.

There may seem to be a contradiction between the idea of creation as giving life and form to preexistent matter—even though that seems implied by the Genesis story with its vague waters already in place—and the orthodox Christian belief that creation was *ex nihilo*, out of nothing. But this may actually be less of a problem than it appears at first glance. I have already suggested that we do not really know what matter is, but only what it does when it takes on form and relationship. If matter is doing nothing and has no coherent relationships, can it be said to exist? Perhaps that problem can be left to other minds. The only universe that could have any meaning for us began when the Holy Spirit aroused it to life. It is this first outrush of the Holy Spirit that established the inseparable union of consciousness with every particle of matter and that is utterly fundamental to the world of form and meaning as we know it.

In the Christian creeds, the Spirit is the "Lord and Giver of Life." Rather than calling the Spirit the third person of the Trinity, it might be better to call it the innermost person: that which in creation is most subtle, pervasive, and energizing, guiding life and its evolution from within. In our personal spiritual life, or in the life of the church, it is often the Holy Spirit that is known first. The way of the Spirit is the personal way, the way of experience, the way of initiation, that begins with the glory of God spread over the Earth, as the waters cover the sea, and is also sown over the fields of the world and cast into the hearts of persons, where they then reflect that glory. We hear the Spirit as a quiet voice deep within us, "interceding for us with sighs too deep for words" (Rom. 8:20). We can see the life of the Spirit radiating in the lives of others; in wanting to know where the joy and power in their lives come from, we may be led to Christ and his church.

The second Outpouring is that of the Logos, the Creative Word of God, also known as the *Nous* or Mind of God and, by Christians, as the Christ. Its meaning for us here and now in this world is particularly revealed in the life and teaching of Jesus—he who lived, taught, and was crucified under Pontius Pilate in Roman Palestine. The word *Christ* is, literally, Greek for the Hebrew-based word *Messiah* or "Anointed One," for anointing was the way of making a king in ancient Israel—the sublime redeemer-king prophesied at the time of Jesus. But in Christian usage, *Christ* has come to refer to the divine and universal significance of what Jesus was.

The second Outpouring is considered an aspect of creation. This is the Logos, which is translated as the "Word" in the famous first chapter of St. John's Gospel: "In the beginning was the Word, and the Word was with God, and the Word was God. The same was in the beginning with God. All things were made by him; and without him was not anything made that was made. In him was life; and the life was the light of men." Essentially, the Logos, or the Christ, is the divine power that gives form to the matter that the Holy Spirit has quickened with life and consciousness. In its mighty presence, the now-lively waves of the primordial sea become solid, cohering into planets, mountains, trees, women, and men.

The Nicene Creed further says of Christ: "Who for us men and for our salvation came down from heaven and was incarnate of the Holy Spirit and the Virgin Mary and was made man. . . ." This is the sublime heart of the parallelism between the story of the second Outpouring and the mystery of the Christ in the Jesus of history; it is the crux of the myth that is also true. Viewing the Christmas story as a model of the second Outpouring, we see the Logos taking on material expression in the Virgin's womb and as the Babe in the manger, giving form to matter that the Holy Spirit has aroused to inchoate life. In this myth, a mysterious visitor declares to Mary, "And behold, you will conceive in your womb and bear a son, and you shall call his name Jesus," but Mary protests that she has no husband. Then the mighty archangel says to the Virgin, "The Holy Spirit will come upon you, and the power of the Most High will overshadow you; therefore the child to be born will be called holy, the Son of God" (Luke 1:31, 35).

The womb of the Virgin Mary represents matter in its unformed "virgin" state yet already touched by the Spirit. Her otherwise untouched flesh symbolizes the substance that the Logos took on in order to make the worlds in which he would ultimately—in his earthly manifestation—appear as human. In the Catholic version of this myth-cycle, the wonderful transformation of virgin matter by the Spirit and by the Word is consummated in the Assumption of the Blessed Virgin Mary into heaven. This mystery reveals vivified matter and awakened humanity to be—when immaculate and perfected—the equal of anything in the supernal realms. Indeed, Mary is said to have been crowned Queen of Heaven.

The female figure of Wisdom is the Book of Proverbs represents the Blessed Virgin Mary and unformed matter. This is not the inert matter of science, but Theosophical matter which is always conjoined with rudimentary consciousness, its glorious mission articulated in its dark, innate desire to pattern itself according to the wisdom of the atoms or of the flesh. This is the Wisdom of Proverbs 8, which was "set up, at the first, before the beginning of the earth," a co-worker with the Creator: "Then I was beside him, like a master workman; and I was daily his delight, rejoicing before him always, rejoicing in his inhabited world and delighting in the sons of men"; and still with us, perhaps incognito, in the faces and voices of those we pass by: "Wisdom cries aloud in the street, in the markets she raises her voice. . . ." (Prov. 1:20).

Surely Wisdom still cries out for recognition of her own creative truth, wanting people to know and do what is right about matter and the intricacies of life to which it leads. She still sends out her serving girls to call from the highest towers of the city for us to come to the feast of true life with its mixed wine (Prov. 9:2). So the coming together of matter and spirit—of the Creator God and the Virgin—is not just a union of consciousness with that which is totally chaotic and unalive. Instead, it is a union of *two* kinds of consciousness—that of matter and that of spirit—for their mutual fulfillment, even as male and female have ever yearned for one another. In other words, creation is not so much a making as it is a marriage.

According to another text this remarkable and mysterious Wisdom, feminine co-creator with God, was sent forth from the heavens into the heat of midday on earth to toil and teach in her own way, so that we "may learn what is pleasing to [God]: for she knows and understands all things, and she will guide [us] wisely in [our] actions" (Apocrypha: Wisdom 9: 10-11). Perhaps, like Isis, Wisdom now takes the guise of many or all women, or of nature as the daughter of God, or of the church as the bride of Christ—toiling, suffering, teaching both with and without words in the form of this marketwoman, that mother, this wife, that ancient sea, this shadow in the forest, that flight of birds sacred to her.

Mother Wisdom, personified in the Blessed Virgin Mary and also representing *prima materia*, the first and virgin matter of creation, is like *maya*, the phenomenal world, or *Shakti*, the consort-goddess as divine creative power, in Hinduism. She is also the Void that is infinite *prajna*, or wisdom, in Buddhism and the Taoist Mother of the Ten Thousand Things. In all these roles, which in the end are the same role, she is virgin—for material creation is always changing and always fresh. Forms rise and fall like birds flying through the air, leaving no tracks in anything that would be hard and solid forever, and even universes appear and then wink out. Yet like a dream, like a glittering snowfall, each form is wonderful and precious and an emblem of eternity.

The assimilation of the Blessed Virgin Mary with virgin matter, giving the latter a personal name and form, correlates well with the contemporary Gaia hypothesis that conceives of the earth as a mysteriously conscious entity with its own purposes and methods. It therefore wonderfully relates esoteric Christianity to an important modern paradigm expressed in contemporary goddess religion and in deep ecology with its passion for living lightly on the land. Those who honor Our Lady will have profound respect for these values, for in honoring all that grows and blooms, all with fin or fur, one also honors her. Yet she also manifested as a maiden in a town of ancient Palestine, so the highways and byways of human civilization, unimmaculate as they often may be, are not alien to her. Nor would esoteric Christianity, unlike some partisans of the goddess, put her at odds with the Sky-Father, for in our view both together parent the wondrous child.

Finally, the third Outpouring, that of the Father, the First Person of the Trinity, is regarded by the esoteric tradition as of a different nature than the others, in that it is not part of the primordial making of suns and worlds and sentient beings in whom dance life and mind. What remains is the full spiritual completion of creation. In Scripture, the First Person is said to be the "Father of Spirits" (Heb. 12:9) and the "God of the Spirits of all flesh" (Num. 16:22).[1] The gift the Father outpours is the divine Spirit as true self, as the dazzling dark within from which stems all our energy and joy. While that Presence is of course ever nearer than hands and feet, its realization is rare and only latent in most of us. So this gift is understood and fully received only by advanced souls high on the course of evolution back to the Halls of Light, where the secrets of all hearts—including the secret Presence—will be made known.

The Trinity and its Outpourings are also understandable in terms of the Hindu formula, which says that Brahman, the Absolute, is *Sat-Chit-Ananda*, "Being-Mind-Joy." Clearly these fit very well if we think of the Father as the source and epitome of Being, the Son as the Mind or Logos of creation, and the Holy Spirit as the Lord and Giver of Life, which at its pinnacle is sheer joyous energy. The Holy Spirit, as the first Outpouring, is a wave of simple joy, a ripple of holy laughter, vibrating through the still waters of unformed matter. We began, in other words, as joy; our deepest level next to the universal divine nature, or *atman*, is as joy becoming a separate joy. Next follows the forming creative mind and finally, the Lord who makes us aware of the inward divinity that is our true nature, long veiled.

It is in Jesus, who gave a human smile to the Christ or Logos, that these great mysteries are seen most clearly by Christians. Jesus was filled with the energy of the Holy Spirit; he lived with the Father intimately, and as he taught and healed he gave form to the words and deeds which revealed him to be a Maker, in whom all things might well have been made. Then he lived out the myth that was true, once and for always, on the Cross and in the Tomb.

3

JESUS AND THE NEVER-ENDING STORY: FROM EDEN TO ETERNITY

When we consider Christ's life on earth as Jesus, we may ask ourselves why the mysteries related to the Outpourings, especially the second, are unveiled to us through the life of a man of modest background who lived in a remote and turbulent province of the Roman Empire. Why through a country preacher who, humanly speaking, might well have been long since forgotten?

The story of Jesus helps us to deal with our human condition of being both flesh and spirit, the products of creation. The combination of matter and consciousness creates wonderful and infinite possibilities for demonstrating the splendor of reality. Yet it also contains inherent contradictions that we are apt to interpret as evil. To put it succinctly, God can become manifest only by accepting limitation. That limitation is a sacrifice for the sake of something greater, and in every sacrifice there is pain. That which was whole is cut up and divided; that which had been infinite is contained; and that which had known the abundance of eternity now suffers deprivation.

The sufferings of Christ reflect the sufferings of

the Logos in emptying itself into matter and taking form, for form does not have the quickness and the freedom of thought. It is restricted by time and space and the laws of nature which say, You can go so far and no farther.

In the Bible, this restriction for the sake of the expression of divine infinity first appears in the Hebrew Scriptures called the Old Testament. Christians owe Judaism an immense debt for the crucial background these texts provide to the story of Jesus, who was himself Jewish.

These Hebrew Scriptures tell us that God selected one small nation from among all the peoples of Earth for a special mission, one that would bring them as much suffering as honor. The founders of that nation—Abraham, his son Isaac, his grandson Jacob or "Israel," and their wives and children—were not saints or paragons of virtue. They were earthy, sometimes deceitful heads of shepherding clans wandering on the outskirts of the great civilizations of Egypt and Mesopotamia. That they were chosen above all others shows that God can reach and transform even unpromising material.

The descendants of those founders, or patriarchs, journeyed to Egypt during a famine and stayed there as slaves for four hundred years. After that span of time, God again reached out to one of them who was to be their leader, Moses, speaking to him through a burning bush that was not consumed. Out of this bush came the mysterious words, "I am that I am" (Ex. 3:14). Moses confronted the pharaoh and then took his people into freedom through the miraculously parted waters of the Red Sea by way of Mt. Sinai, where they received the divine Law by which they were to live. Eventually, after many trials, God gave them the land of Palestine, where they established a kingdom the greatest rulers of which were David and Solomon. A temple was built at the capital, Jerusalem, where priests offered rituals and sacrifices according to the divine instructions delivered on Mt. Sinai. The realm went through victories, divisions, and defeats, including the exile of its leaders in Babylon.

During this time some people, including a few kings, remained faithful to God, though many served the agricultural gods of the land instead, such as Baal and Astarte, who seemed more congenial to their agrarian way of life. But there were those called the Prophets—Amos, Hosea, Isaiah, Jeremiah, and others—who insisted that their God was not merely a tribal but a universal God whose concerns were far greater than Baal's. This God was concerned with the working out of justice in the vast arena of all human history leading up to a last day of judgment and power.

Thus, the tribal affairs involving Abraham and Moses were only a beginning. The Hebrew Scriptures bring history up to a few centuries before the time of Jesus; but the end to which they point, the fulfillment of all the promises contained in world history, has yet to come.

This story can be interpreted both as history and as allegory. First, even though some of it may be legendary, it is based in history and forces us to confront the spiritual meaning of living in time. It tells us that one way in which God constricts God for the sake of expression is by working through human history—and the terrible pain and flawed characters of which it is partly composed. The story puts hope not outside of this world in some otherworldly realm, but ahead of us in historical time, and tells us we will only fulfill this hope by working for justice through the wars and messy politics of real human experience. On this level, the esoteric perspective reminds us that there is a secret thread running through human history, the thread of a divine purpose leading to a now-hidden consummation at the end of time brighter than anything we can imagine. This thread runs deep in the heart of things, even when they seem most discouraging and grim, and in the end makes all the suffering worthwhile for those who can see that their own pilgrimage runs parallel with that purpose and remains true to it. This is the pilgrimage of the Path.

This historical narrative projecting hope into the future is distinctive enough to make Judaism and Christianity an excellent foundation for spirituality in the modern world. We in the twentieth century are intensely aware of history in all its horror and hope, and it helps to know that good can come out of the historical process. At the same time, the biblical sources themselves may not fully articulate all dimensions of human hope. Theosophical and esoteric traditions tell us that, in the end, some hopes will be fulfilled that are not explicit in the Judeo-Christian Scriptures: hopes for vegetarianism, for environmental health, and for enhanced consciousness on all planes of being.

Secondly, the story can also be interpreted as allegory. In the Gospel narratives of Jesus, the Kingdom has both historical *and* allegorical strands; it is both a known thing and a secret, as was the messianic calling of its proclaimer. Jesus asked, "Who do you say that I am?" and Peter boldly answered, "You are the Christ, the Son of the Living God," whereupon Jesus "strictly charged the disciples to tell no one that he was the Christ" (Matt. 16:16, 20).

Allegorical interpretations have been made by many ancient and medieval writers, both Jewish and Christian, and by more recent authorities like Emanuel Swedenborg and Geoffrey Hodson. For example, Hodson says that the unconsumed burning bush Moses saw represents the atma, the divine within beyond birth or death, and that the crossing of the Red Sea is an image of the inner spiritual ascent to God through much hardship. There seems to be no reason why both the historical and the allegorical meanings of these events should not be valid, since most of what happens in history—and in our own lives—is capable of bearing both meanings simultaneously. Thus, these are myths that also happen to be true. (Admittedly, it takes faith to find the allegory and secret thread of divine purpose in the sordid political affairs and international betrayals and wars that fill our newspapers and newscasts today. But things were no different in the days of the patriarchs and prophets, who surely needed just as much faith as we.)

For Christians, the Hebrew story has additional significance in that it is necessary to the future role of Jesus. He has traditionally been called prophet, priest, and king, for in him Christians see a consummate expression of all three roles: like the prophets, he spoke on behalf of justice and the poor; like the priests of old who offered animal victims, he offered himself as a sacrifice; and like David and the other Hebrew kings, he ruled over the inward Kingdom of God and would return as outward ruler of the completed Kingdom at the end of time. From an esoteric point of view, Jesus was so in tune with the inner rhythms of the world that he manifested the second Outpouring or creative mind of God in a special way. He was in harmony with the acts of God in history as well as with the inner life of the world, and no less with the cosmic rhythms of manifestation and withdrawal out of which this and all other worlds have flowed.

THE ESOTERIC INTERPRETATION OF THE CRUCIFIXION

The wise speak of Jesus' crucifixion on the Cross of Calvary as the crucifixion of the Creative Word of God on the Cross of matter—as symbolic, in other words, of the sacrifice God must make in order to enter into matter and make it the universe. God within the material world also subtly transforms it to demonstrate the glory with which God invests it; for, as the myth tells us, God is not ultimately killed by matter but instead gives it new life. The quickening of barren branches every spring mirrors in nature the Resurrection of he who seemed dead and buried within the womb of the earth, yet who ascends in glory. It also mirrors the Assumption into heaven of she who, mythically speaking, first gave him entry into the realm of matter.

Matter must not be thought of as inherently evil in itself; it is capable of splendor and holiness as great as that of any plane of being. However, for its splendor to be revealed, matter must first be properly joined with consciousness and with all the other planes so that light shines through them unimpeded down to the physical plane. Then, there is always descent and ascent, involution and evolution. The one who knows what it means to be crucified on the Cross of matter—trapped in the excruciating contradictions of being a spiritual consciousness imprisoned in flesh—must find the way up to where the sun and sky can be seen. That is the course of initiation. In the esoteric tradition, what is outwardly spoken of as salvation is a process of initiation parallel to that of a lodge or mystery religion. But, for esoteric Christians, the model, guide, and chief initiator is Jesus the Christ himself.

How are we, as was he, crucified on the Cross of matter? And how are the initiated brought back from it?

To get at these questions, consider the nature of what we call evil. Evil must first of all be that which we sense ought *not* to be, especially when it involves pain and suffering. In the words of St. Paul, it is the "mystery of iniquity" (2 Thess. 2:7); in those of Jesus, the "abomination of desolation . . . standing where it ought not" (Mark 13:14). Evil seems to be present when a child who, instead of playing happily, suffers terrible abuse or wasting disease; when a city is leveled by war or earthquake; or when the life of any human or animal is arbitrarily cut short. It spreads its most potent dread in the form of the fear that cosmic law is, in fact, irrational; that suffering strikes good and bad and indifferent alike without reason; and that, in the end, the universe gives cause for nothing but the deepest despair.

Yet if anything is clear both from esoteric traditions and from everyday experience, it is that the key to distinguishing evil from other eventualities is in the breakdown of oneness into many things when matter and consciousness are joined. The pulverizing of a piece of inert matter like a rock does not affect us as does the destruction of the organized mixture of consciousness and matter that is a dog or a donkey. Our awareness of the constriction, pain, or destruction of anything that embodies the finite manifestations of consciousness—in other words, of any being we can see, touch, and love—seems close to the dark heart of evil as we understand it.

Paradoxically, this kind of constriction comes about when existence opens out into dualism and multiplicity. When the One is one alone, nothing can confine it; but duality engenders not only greater diversity of expression, but also limitations on each of the two entities—and how much greater the limits become as two increases to ten thousand and then into infinity! Two or more inherently give rise to conflict. This truth is symbolized by the story of Satan's rebellion against God (Luke 10:18, Rev. 20:1-3), so well dramatized in Milton's *Paradise Lost*, which mythologizes the origin of evil in the One becoming two, and then three, and then ten thousand things.

Rebellion is also reflected in the story of the Garden of Eden, in which our primal parents disobeyed God, eating of the tree of the knowledge of good and evil. That is, they incorporated the possibilities inherent in multiplicity, including their own role as separate sentient beings capable of making choices. Yet God in the garden stayed close to the first couple, and they—like us—did not *have* to know other than God. We were intended to have knowledge, not of good and evil, but only of the good and of the God who made us and walked in the garden with us in the cool of the day (Gen. 2:8, 3:8). Eden is in the east—the direction of light and initiation, representing all that is good about being man and woman, individual and clothed in material garments. It and the Gardener are all that we need to know; but that other tree is unavoidably planted there as well, for Eden's orchard is a seemingly harmless reflection of multiplicity, and so also of the possibility of choice, for good or ill.

Exploring the symbolism of Jesus' crucifixion can help us understand the nature of duality. First, his death on the Cross represents the pain—the suffering, the constriction, the evil—inherent in the manifested world of finite forms whose outward face is the many different shapes of matter. He suffered, in other words, because he was in a physical body which,

65

being limited, can only be in one place at a time—
and therefore was capable of being nailed onto a
Cross on a particular Friday morning. He also suffered because he was at large in a world of men and
women whose consciousness was severely con-
strained by their own immersion in matter—that is,
by the fears, desires, and profoundly clouded sight
that led them to do an evil deed for what they no
doubt considered good reasons. Jesus' excruciating
death was a consequence, then, of *our* knowing good
and evil, and he had to suffer for our knowledge even
if he himself knew only the good.

It is important to realize that, as the Christian
tradition has always insisted, Jesus died an innocent
victim who in no way deserved the cruel and humili-
ating torture to which he was subjected. You may
consider the questions of karma, sin, and guilt, but
Jesus in this life did nothing to warrant the fate that
came his way. He is a supreme illustration of the
fact that, in this world, the innocent do suffer and
the guiltless are punished at the hands of the wicked.
Jesus died a horrible death as did the piteous victims of a thousand massacres and extermination
camps.

Of course, our karma extends beyond the limits
of a single life in this world. We are also deeply affected by the karma of our previous lives and by the
karma of the larger groups—the families, nations, and
worlds—to which we belong. The orthodox Christian tradition would not say that Jesus had lived previously on Earth. On the other hand, it does emphasize his interconnection—call it karmic—with the

world as a whole. He suffered, it is said, for the sins of the whole world; and by enduring that suffering, he paid the price for our sin and removed its immense debt. Those who accept that Jesus has thus redeemed them, while they still may have their own individual karma for which to atone, are no longer burdened by the collective sin of the world but can set out on their path, joyous and free.

This language of law and finance—"atonement," "redemption," "paying the penalty due"—in which Christian doctrine is often expressed seems crude or even offensive to many modern people. Yet it reveals profound esoteric truths. Chief among them is the interrelatedness of all earthly beings, wherein the evil of one can indeed inflict pain on another, and the good of one can relieve another's pain.

THE EFFECTS OF ESOTERIC KNOWLEDGE

The Gospels also say that Jesus knew remarkable things about the intimate lives of others and about what was to come. Sometimes we ask ourselves questions about these matters. What, if any, are the limits to what *we* can know, do, feel, suffer, love, or share? Can we really merge with someone else's life? Can we really bear another's burdens and take on another's pain? Can we elevate ourselves to a level where consciousness can do seemingly magical things, even lifting us out of our physical body and its limitations? Can we raise our consciousness to a virtuoso level where we know far more than the ordinary person and can even see into the recesses of the past and the future?

Jesus often called himself the "Son of Man"—a phrase more commonly used in the Gospels than "Son of God." Whatever else it may mean, this mysterious expression reflects a rich sense of his common humanity with all whom he met and of his being a focal point for the ever-turning cycle of human affairs. As the old Christmas hymn puts it, "The hopes and fears of all the years/Are met in thee tonight"; or, "The world turns, the cross stands still," according to the motto of the venerable Carthusian order of monks. For Christians, it is indeed as if something stands still when we look at Jesus as portrayed in the Gospel stories. They let us see the timeless now, the eternal reality and meaning of events. When Jesus holds a child and says, "Of such is the Kingdom of Heaven," he speaks of *all* children . . . for, as the Gospel states, "Inasmuch as ye have done it unto one of the least of these my brethren, ye have done it unto me" (Matt. 25:40). When he becomes the innocent victim on the Cross, he is *all* innocent victims. In Christianity, as in all religions, there is a level at which the distinction between one person and another—and even between subject and object—breaks down, and we make the world of meaning as we discover it.

In this world of many parts, the many becomes one when things cohere so smoothly that friction is gone and everything is seen just as it is. So did Jesus often seem to have a relationship of uncanny intimacy with the transient world around him, both human and inanimate. He seems to have had the kind of coordination of mood and muscle that athletes experience, called "runner's high" or being "in the zone." In those magical moments, you almost feel as though you are flying or invisible, able to do anything. On one occasion, after speaking to a synagogue congregation that became hostile, Jesus was able to pass through them without being detained (Luke 4:30). At other times, he could still the waves of a sea or walk on water (Mark 4:35, 6:48). He had the mystic capacity to see all of nature just as it is: the birds of the air and the lilies of the field in all their glory, beyond the splendor of Solomon (Matt. 6:26-30). Nor did Jesus neglect the inner struggles that enabled him to attain those harmonies with the hidden patterns of reality; we are told that he rose long before dawn to pray, and even his disciples did not know where he was (Mark 1:35).

Does esoteric Christianity accept faith in Jesus as Lord and Savior? Yes! For the esoteric Christian, Jesus as Christ represents the highest self: our supreme ideals, visions, and hopes, and the best image of who we are and of the divine within. He represents the pilgrim self that is the ultimate source of all of our highest aspects as they reflect the inner divine, our most authentic personality. For Christians, Jesus is the personification of this inner reality; for he was true to his own best nature, expressed his most authentic personality in innumerable difficult encounters, and—as the historical image of the Christ that dwells within us through our faith (Eph. 3:17)—is the Christian image of the highest virtue possible. To have faith in Jesus is to be true to our best self and our highest ideals, even unto death. With such faith we are like those knights of Arthur's Table who attended mass before setting out on quests, including the quest for the Grail.

Our own inner divinity is lodged in the *monad*[1] or the pilgrim who journeys for no other reason ultimately than self-knowledge. Faith in Jesus helps on this journey, for although the divine is within us, it can seem cloudy and far away; and often the only way we can know what is within is through the reflection of an outer image. In our lack of full, immediate awareness, we want and need intermediaries. It helps to see the divine in particularized forms we can know and love as if we were knowing and loving another, above all in the forms and faces of the world. And it is in Jesus that all these forms are represented: "Inasmuch as you have done it unto one of the least of these my brethren, you have done it unto me." In loving all we love Jesus; in loving Jesus we learn to love all. The great modern mystic Baron von Hügel once said, "I kiss my child not only because I love him, but also in order to love him."

Jesus also acts as a conduit of divine power to the world and is especially well suited to transmit this energy. Just as water flows best in a pipe without rust, and electricity in a conductor without resistance, so do divine energies pass freely through one whose attunement with the people and world around him is so profound that there is no impediment on any level. Many consider that Jesus' transmission of divine power remains available to us even today and is indeed unconditioned by time or space. This transmission over invisible channels or pathways of the spirit can be activated in the present by faith in Jesus, by rituals such as the Eucharist or Holy Communion performed in his name, or even by a picture or a thought of the sage of Galilee.

Jesus' acceptance of his divine purpose enabled him to join with the Second Person of the Divine Trinity and with the Outpourings of the Creative Mind that also works through hidden channels. These channels of divine creativity, like much of the life of Jesus, seem only natural to us because they build from the hidden inside outward. And in the deepest sense they are natural—if we understand nature to include cosmic consciousness.

THE NICENE CREED

The essential teachings of Christianity were set down in the Nicene Creed, which is accepted and used as the basic expression of faith by the major divisions of the Christian church, both Eastern and Western. Its fundamental structure was adopted by the Council of Nicaea in 325 A.D. It was perhaps modified by the Council of Constantinople in 381 A.D. and then was received almost universally in the Church by the sixth century A.D. It is as recited today in the Theosophically related Liberal Catholic Church[2] as follows:

We believe in one God, the Father almighty, maker of heaven and earth and of all things visible and invisible.

And in one Lord, Jesus Christ, the alone-born Son of God; begotten of his Father before all ages, God of God, Light of Light, very God of very God, begotten, not made, being of one substance with the Father, by whom all things were made. Who for us men and for our salvation came down from heaven and was incarnate of the Holy Ghost and the Virgin Mary and was made man. And was crucified also for us; under Pontius Pilate he suffered and was buried. And the third day he rose again according to the Scriptures and ascended into heaven and sitteth on the right hand of the Father. And he shall come again with glory to judge both the quick and the dead; whose kingdom shall have no end.

And we believe in the Holy Ghost, the Lord, the giver of life. Who proceedeth from the Father and the Son, who with the Father and the Son together is worshipped and glorified, who spake by the prophets. We acknowledge one holy catholic and apostolic church. We acknowledge one baptism for the remission of sins. And we look for the resurrection of the dead and the life of the world to come. Amen.

The esoteric as well as the exoteric meaning of Christian faith is implicit in these lines. The first paragraph clearly speaks of the ultimate and fundamental unity of all things in their divine source. This unity will be realized by those who attain it through the last and greatest Outpouring. The last paragraph proclaims faith in the Holy Ghost or Holy Spirit, which is the first Outpouring and still the most active—though inwardly so—of the divine principles at work in the world. The Spirit as Lord and "giver of life" is what separates the living world as it is from simply inert matter. The Holy Spirit operates in co-ordination with the second Outpouring—that of the Creative Mind of God, seen esoterically in Jesus Christ; therefore, the Spirit is "worshipped and glo-rified" together with him and the Father of whom he spoke. Indeed, the Creed informs us that the Spirit was within the entire process of sacred history leading up to the coming of Christ, for it was the Spirit who spoke through the prophets. It was also the Spirit who opened the inner channels, making divine energy available through the church—that is, for all who are open to the influx of divine power originating in the life of Jesus—regardless of time or place. Those channels include baptism "for the re-mission of sins," which can free us to start life anew without inner impediments of past karma, although our karma may still influence the outer conditions of our life. Finally, the esoteric meaning of the "resur-rection of the dead and the life of the world to come" is that in the end, all dualism between thought and feeling and consciousness and matter will be over-come, enabling us to return to our eternal Home in utter unity.

In the second paragraph of the Creed, Jesus comes into the world bearing the nature of the di-vine Christ—the Son of the second Outpouring, the Creative Mind of God—as well as his human nature derived from Mary that represents the material side of reality. Thus, he is a model and precursor of the total overcoming of any dualism between the material and the divine, this unity being supremely evident in his glorious resurrection.

But how much is left unsaid between "and was incarnate of the Holy Ghost and the Virgin Mary and was made man" and "was crucified also for us; under Pontius Pilate he suffered and was buried." The span is thirty years; all the time between Christmas and Good Friday. In this period happened whatever gave the other events their significance. Jesus may not have been the only son born of Mary—the New Testament also refers to his brothers; he may not have been the only person ever born of a virgin; and others certainly suffered under Pontius Pilate, who was well known for his ruthlessness. But what is distinct about Jesus appears in the interval, during the time of his unification with God and the true nature of things in the circumstances of everyday life. It is clear that Jesus was a person completely at ease with the divine and the human and their commingling. Jesus' references to his heavenly Father can seem almost casual and perfunctory. He makes statements such as "Your heavenly Father also will forgive you . . . your Father knows what you need before you ask him. . . ."(Matt. 6:14, 8) in a matter-of-fact way, as though assumed rather than wrought out of the agony of prayer and doubt.

In a way, Jesus is not really different from what we all are: children of God. We all have the divine within; we can all love, heal, and die for others. But

osophy calls the astral, from which came the demons he cast out; and those called the mental, from which his angels came; and those of the Spirit and the Father. Nothing from these inner planes could disrupt the intense joy he felt at being alive, neither unwanted dreams nor waking terrors nor hateful impulses. None of what keeps us dead after we die—the subtle fear and fascination of the other side—had any hold on Jesus at all.

4

IF I BE LIFTED UP:
ALTARS OF THE HEART

According to the Gospel of St. John, the Christ who went up to Calvary and the Cross had earlier said, "And I, if I be lifted up from this earth, will draw all men unto me" (John 12:32). There are those who contend that religion can be held entirely in the realm of ideas or that we at most only need the help of a private practice such as meditation. Such views, like all views on religion, are to be respected and may be right for some people. They may have been right to some extent for Jesus, who did not *need* the external religion of his time and actually directed stinging criticism against its leading practitioners for their ostentation, hypocrisy, and legalism. Yet at the same time, "to fulfill all righteousness," Jesus accepted baptism from the revival preacher John the Baptist, read and preached in synagogues, and praised those who were sincerely devout within the structure of conventional religion. Most profoundly, with respect to Jesus and worship, many Christians find that, in order to touch for themselves the inner freedom that was his, they first need to see him "lifted up" in the form of some kind of picture or symbol—in their hearts, in their minds, before their eyes. They often discover that, beyond their expectations, these signs and symbols offer reminders and stimuli on the psychological level and they also seem to clear inner channels, through the freedom of Jesus, to the Creative Mind of God with which he was united.

That is what Christian worship ought to be about. If it does not liberate, it is worthless. But it *does* liberate, both with and without the help of forms, and by both engaging our bodies and five senses as well as transcending them—for we, like Jesus, are creatures of flesh and blood. It would be strange if worship did not acknowledge this reality by using all the levels of our being: from the physical to the emotional, the image-making astral, the mental, the intuitive, and the divine within. (See Appendix I: The Inner Planes.) It would also be strange—and very unfortunate—if worship did not ultimately unite all levels of being around the divine within, as they were united in Jesus: "There are three that bear witness in earth, the spirit, and the water, and the blood: and these three agree in one" (I John 5:8). A unity of Spirit, flesh, and blood is far healthier, and more like Jesus, than the dualism between spirit and flesh set up by some who consider themselves highly spiritual.

St. Paul speaks of humans as comprised of body, soul, and spirit (*sarx, psyche,* and *pneuma* in Greek)—a trinity, in fact, rather than a duality. The body is of course the flesh, the physical organism in all its wonder and limitations. The soul is the level of mind, intellect, and emotion—what in Theosophy is thought of as our etheric, astral, mental, and intuitive bodies (see appendix). Spirit can be thought of as the atma, the eternal divine essence within. True worship ought to mean using all these aspects of the self combined with action on each level—including physical action—to clear the channels for the light of the atma to shine through all of our being. It can thereby include bodily gestures such as kneeling, taking bread and wine, and going on pilgrimage; it can also mean generating emotional feelings of love and devotion; and it can mean building thought-forms with the mind as channels of energy from the eternal source.

The validity of worship should not be judged by worldly standards such as whether the efficacy of prayer, spiritual healings, and the like can be scientifically measured or confirmed. Actually, all worship is *primarily* done on the inner planes of feeling, imagination, and consciousness. These have a causal relation to the visible physical world, as it does to them. This is why prayers and sacraments do sometimes effect outer results and why physical means—gestures such as kneeling, or the spoken words of ritual, or the architecture of churches and temples—can assist in the workings of the inner planes. But this relationship between the inner planes and the physical world is a complex and sometimes indirect one, influenced by factors well beyond ordinary human understanding. It is rather like the way sea and atmosphere create weather over the ocean: certainly there are intricate interconnections, but also very powerful independent currents in both elements that have dynamics of their own.

Worship therefore works and constructs its own structures as much on the inner planes as it does outwardly and cannot be judged solely by outer effects. More importantly, it has assistance from entities on the inner planes, especially the spirits of saints and the presences we call angels, and benefits—or at least interacts with—other inhabitants of those planes, living and deceased. Consequently, a person sensitive to the inner planes may see colors and structures of astral or mental material gather around a place of worship, revealing something of its nature and direction.

BUILDING AN ESOTERIC CATHEDRAL

Worship builds a structure for communication with the atma on the level of the inner planes—we can think of it as a cathedral we construct out of the bricks and mortar of thought-forms. In a conventional Christian service, the reading of the Scripture builds the foundations of such a structure on the astral level, since Jesus and others in the scriptural stories had many dealings with that plane and its entities. The Creed and the sermon, then, because they challenge our minds on profound levels, add the equivalent of walls and soaring buttresses on the mental plane. The anthem or the offertory raise our thoughts to the intuitive or buddhic level of wordless realization, as though raising the cathedral's altar. Finally, the climax of the service, such as the consecration and receiving of Holy Communion or

deep meditation at the highest point, opens a conduit of light-transmitting power and benediction directly from the divine, the atma, the Blessed Trinity.
We may think of it as a splendid rose window above
the inner cathedral altar that casts radiant beams of
light down on the congregation.

Angelic beings from the mental plane and astral entities worship along with humans. The angels
enjoy the warmth of worship and the beautiful
thought-forms it creates; out of their mercy they help
spread divine light and energy throughout the church
and its surroundings. Visitors from the astral plane
may be there more out of need, or even misguided
desire, yet they must not be forgotten, for they are
among those to whom the church must communi-
cate the love of God and the saving grace of Christ.

Too often, human congregations are unaware of
the astral beings in their midst—although they may
be numerous, perhaps even outnumbering the incarnate worshippers. This lack of awareness is very
unfortunate. We need to be conscious of these invisible guests, because a few may be able to do serious harm if we ignore them when we are open to
spiritual influx. More importantly, though, these are
beings in need of our prayers and radiation of love.
Roman Catholics pray for the souls in Purgatory,
which corresponds to what we have called the astral
plane. But this is not some distant place; rather, it is
here now in our midst, its needful inhabitants as near
as our thoughts.

In the same way, heaven, or Devachan—the
mental plane of our thought-form cathedral—is im-

mediately present in and with us in worship. It only takes a meditative awareness to know that this is true. Even in the humblest church, there is a splendor behind the symbols and in the eyes of the faithful that is the light of heaven.

The world of worship should be thought of as being one with the world of consciousness, which is just as real as the material world but of an entirely different nature. Consciousness is hardly nearer to the dense physical level, except through subtle influences, than high clouds are near the plains; but it is no less real than physical phenomena. We may have thoughts as grand as Plato's and feelings as rich or poignant as those of Shakespeare, and these thoughts and feelings are not less real because they can't be weighed or measured. The consciousness/worship level has its own specific ways of knowing, modes of communication, and extraordinary states of being. During worship, lives can be changed and divine grace can filter down—or burst into the mind like a subtle-plane explosion—though there may be only scant awareness of it in our ordinary state, the transformative effects arising only gradually or perhaps not until later.

Esoteric Christian worship is not based on the concept of Jesus as merely an external God, whether harsh or loving, or as just an after-death savior, but as a person of inner freedom whose life we can share here and now. His state of freedom can be reached with the help of pathways cut by thought, word, and deed through all these planes. Of course, many Christians who do not think of themselves as esotericists also have this kind of understanding of their relationship to Jesus. The esotericist is simply more likely than others to look at the nature of the path, its geography, and the tools required. Christian worship that learns and uses inner-planes tools, as well as grasps the concept of inwardness, may be called esoteric. It would be a travesty to regard something as subtle and transcendent as the divine and the inner planes as subject to scientific or technological investigation. Yet, as spiritual teachers of all religions and ages have known, there are structured techniques which, if practiced with deep reverence and humility, can help us in approaching God and the inner pathways through prayer, meditation, formal worship, and sacrament. But the esoteric spiritual builder must approach the work with profound reverence and humility, as an act of devotion and service, and with no thought of arrogance or superior wisdom. Otherwise, the adoration of the simplest ordinary believer would be better.

All religions have a place for acts of devotion and for understanding them on different levels. Historical religions such as Judaism, Hinduism, Buddhism, Christianity, and Islam cannot be merely constructed of subjective attitudes; they require an outward means of expression. Without formal ideas, practices, and institutions to help followers realize their inward experience and carry its essence from one generation to another, it is highly unlikely that these religions would have continued as historically important forces over the millennia. These practices are what people *do* when they go to temple and church: they bow; kneel; sing hymns; look at altars, pictures, stained-glass windows, and statues of saints; stand and sit; hear sermons; and pray together or quietly in their hearts.

It is unclear to most of us just how much of our personal concept of God is the result of our conditioned thinking and how much of it is real or true. We probably project onto God far more of the names and forms of what we worship than we realize. There is nothing wrong with this as long as we realize that we shape our God out of our limited understanding in an effort to comprehend intelligently that which is above us. This effort is what worship is about from the esoteric point of view: For on the deepest level all is God, including the light of consciousness in our minds and the forms we make out of our thoughts, and are therefore ways that God is self-knowing. God manifests all these names and forms in divine play and, as in all real play, joy is in it. Jesus himself allowed God to be known to him as "Father," and as he manifested God, God gave Jesus another great name and form, calling him Jesus the Christ.

How then is the house of worship built? The outer form of worship works in several ways. First, it can provide what mystics call a one-pointed focus. Our inner disposition to worship is strengthened by points of visual, audial, and mental attention that quiet the activity of the "monkey mind," which otherwise always jumps from one thing to another. This quieting enables the mind to take time out from its ceaseless activity just to be itself—pure consciousness open to the influxes of the universal; full of its being, mind, and joy—as was Jesus. To gaze on the Cross of Christ or an image of the Blessed Virgin, to contemplate the holy mysteries of the mass, or to listen to the joyous sounds of gospel music are appropriate ways to begin sharing in the openness of Jesus.

Second, a good service or ritual enables us to lose ourselves in something larger than our own egos. The rite can become like a great dance in which we know the joy that comes with being swept along by music, movement, and beauty. The sacred action can then inwardly lift us out of the bondage of our own time and place to the worship of the whole church past, present, and future. Then, finally, we are a part of the dance of the planets and the music of the spheres and are one with the stillness at the center of the dance.

THE NATURE OF RELIGIOUS RITES

Religious rites are a way of connecting with the past, both of the religion and of our own life. Religion has been called a "ritual perpetuation of the past," and while that may not completely define religion, it is certainly a significant part of it. Consciously or unconsciously, many people participate in religion because it connects them to the history of their nation, ethnic group, or family, or to joyous moments in their own past. Religious services are full of "condensed symbols" of the past. These reminders are just enough to jog memories and trigger associations: the tiny bit of bread and wine or grape juice used in the Holy Communion reminds us of Jesus' Last Supper with his disciples; the peculiar rhythms of a few bars of religious music can call up an ethnic heritage; the Cross tells its own symbolic story.

From an esoteric viewpoint these rites are apertures to the work on the inner planes. Symbols such as the Cross, the bread and wine of the Eucharist, or the sounds of a hymn can provide means for the energies of Christ to reach us in two ways: First, on the inner planes they can serve as channels that convey heavenly power. Second, our responses to what is occurring create thought-forms that prepare places within our consciousness for their reception. Thought-forms convey energies generated on the astral and mental levels that are created by certain kinds of thoughts with their associated feelings. Annie Besant and C.W. Leadbeater, in a celebrated book entitled *Thought-Forms*,[1] have provided illustrated descriptions of the subtle energies that surround someone who is, for example, inflamed by anger or exalted by magnificent music. These forms are very impressive. They certainly correlate with the subtle energies activated and directed by Christian worship, as Leadbeater has described them in *The Science of the Sacraments*.[2]

As an example of thought-forms, let us consider what Leadbeater says about the confession of sins and the receiving of divine forgiveness in church. Although practices such as formal absolution or pronouncement of God's forgiveness may vary from one denomination to another, certainly the idea of confession and forgiveness is common to virtually all Christians.

Leadbeater interprets sin in esoteric terms, speaking of it as

> anything that is against the divine Will—that is, against the current of evolution. If a man intentionally does something to hold back evolution, either his own or that of somebody else, then emphatically he is doing wrong. . . . When he does or thinks evil, he wrenches himself away from the direction of this spiritual current [evolution], and thereby sets up a definite *strain* in etheric, astral and mental matter, so that he is no longer in harmony with nature, no longer a helping but a hindering force, a snag in the river of life. This strain, or cross-twist, almost entirely arrests his progress for the time, and renders it impossible for him to profit by all the impulses of good influence which are constantly rushing along the current of the stream of which we have spoken. Before he can do any real good for himself or anyone else, he must straighten out that distortion, and come into harmony with nature, and so be once more fully amenable to good influence, and able to take advantage of the many and valuable aids which are so lavishly provided for him.[3]

Leadbeater then tells us that the church, through its ministers, pours out absolving force over the congregation in worship, which can "straighten out this tangle in higher matter." But we can only truly receive this absolving force when we open ourselves to its power by sincere confession and the desire to amend our life. The energy of this action, he says, stamps the energy of the penitent's higher Self upon the personality, and clears

> the channel connecting it with the Greater Self. The power of God stimulates the Divine Image within each of us to impress Itself more definitely on the personality, and in forcing itself down it clears out any kinks in the connecting channel between the lower and higher selves—between the individual and God. Thus the Life of the Logos—the evolutionary stream—can again flow smoothly through the man. He is no longer a snag in the stream, because he has been put right in his relation with his Maker.[4]

If this perspective is possible in the confession and forgiveness of sins, how much more could be accomplished in the great corporate acts of Christian worship—singing hymns, praying together, hearing sermons, and receiving sacraments such as Holy Communion. The forms of Christian worship are immensely varied among its many traditions and denominations. Following are descriptions of the esoteric aspects of different forms of worship. These, except for Leadbeater's, are imaginative constructions on my part; I claim no clairvoyant ability.

In the typical Protestant service with its majestic or warmly devotional hymns, Scripture reading, pastoral prayer, sermon, anthem, offertory, and recessional, I picture a splendid dome of clear light built over the congregation on the mental plane. This dome is formed by the purity of feeling the service creates in most of the participants and by the simple attention to God expressed in the unambiguous plain words of the reading and preaching. There is a subtle diversity of vibrations, like soft eddies in a still pond, which move within that clarity; these are the diverse responses of individuals to the words of worship. If the preaching and emotional tone become fiery, then more colors arise, usually in solid but vivid hues— red, blue, purple, green—reflecting energy and passionate commitment, a sense of sin and of God's overcoming it, and spiritual growth. Finally, a soft shattering of the light at the end of the service indicates that the congregation is breaking up and going in separate, but one hopes committed, ways. However, beings on the astral plane who approach this service are less well served, except when someone is especially sensitive to their presence and needs. The words of preaching sound very far-away to the ears of astral beings, and their minds are not well attuned to philosophical thought; they desire only the warmth of divine grace through channels they can comprehend and the healing power of love.

In contrast, a very different structure is built during the celebration of a traditional Roman Catholic mass. The esoteric significance of the mass is well described in a famous passage by Leadbeater:

My attention was first called to this matter by watching the effect produced by the celebration of the Mass in a Roman Catholic church in a little village in Sicily. Those who know that most beautiful of islands will understand that one does not meet with the Roman Catholic Church there in its most intellectual form, and neither the Priest nor the people could be described as especially highly developed; yet the quite ordinary celebration of the Mass was a magnificent display of the application of occult force.

At the moment of consecration the Host glowed with the most dazzling brightness; it became in fact a veritable sun to the eye of the clairvoyant, and as the Priest lifted it above the heads of the people I noticed that two distinct varieties of spiritual force poured forth from it, which might perhaps be taken as roughly corresponding to the light of the sun and streamers of his corona. The first (let us call it Force A) rayed out impartially in all directions upon the people in the church; indeed, it penetrated the walls of the church as though they were not there, and influenced a considerable section of the surrounding country. . . . [The] second force was called into activity only in response to a strong feeling of devotion on the part of an individual. At the elevation of the Host all members of the congregation duly prostrated themselves—some apparently as a mere mat-

ter of habit, but some also with a strong up-
welling of deep devotional feeling. The effect
as seen by clairvoyant sight was most striking
and profoundly impressive, for to each of these
latter there darted from the uplifted Host a ray
of fire, which set the higher part of the astral
body of the recipient glowing with the most
intense ecstasy. . . .[5]

Of course, there may be significant variations
from what has been described on both the Protestant and the Catholic sides. Consider, for example,
the special case represented by a meeting of the Society of Friends or Quakers. Participants sit in a
meeting-house room—usually very plain and func-
tional in design—in perfect silence until someone is
led by the Spirit to stand and speak a few words,
pray, or lead a hymn. This worship has no outward
sacraments, water baptism, or holy communion with
bread and wine; instead, it is marked by a sense of
the presence of God within—the "inner light"— and
no less by a tenderness toward the presence of God
in all persons and places. The experience of this
form of worship has led Quakers to conduct world-
wide ministries on behalf of peace and reconciliation between groups and nations. On the mental
plane, a Friends' meeting might create a structure of
a rich warm hemisphere of gray flecked with gold.
Somber gray is a traditional color of Quaker garb, but
this gray is full of soundless shifts of light and tone
throughout the texture and becomes more shot with
gold as the meeting progresses. On the astral plane,

there is relatively little activity at a Quaker meeting, generally because of a lack of esoteric awareness on the part of many contemporary Friends. However, one can sense a few astral entities creeping toward the edges of the meeting's canopy and then discovering with delight the golden healing warmth hidden in the gray.

The Eastern Orthodox liturgy, a Catholic form of service, suggests the desire to make physically visible what is transpiring on the astral and mental planes by intentionally creating sacramental thought-forms that channel divine energy from the heart of God. The actual correspondence may not always be exact, since no human craft or art could completely reproduce the worlds of the inner planes; but the feeling of color, richness, and unity-in-diversity is there. In Eastern Orthodoxy, the often-concealed altar behind the *iconostasis*, a screen covered with icons and pictures of saints, is like the innermost eternal realm of pneuma, spirit, the atma, the God within. This power seems to radiate through the saints with their luminous eyes as though they were beings in the heaven of the mental plane, or Devachan. As the service progresses with its mystical and unforgettable music, its richly-robed clergy moving with the slowness of ancient ritual, and its billowing clouds of incense, a dome of silvery-blue light that merges upward into gold is formed above the congregation, like the onion-shaped domes atop many Orthodox churches. The structure is so exalted that it barely touches the earth, and not all present are able to perceive it directly. Out of this covering falls a fine mist-like rain of transparent grace which is able to touch, lightly or profoundly, the lives of those beneath it, including the many astral forms who are drawn to this form of ritual.

These examples make it evident that a service of worship is like an orchestration of symbols. Messages reach us through several senses simultaneously to provide an environment rich in the symbols of the religion and the reality behind them. Entering this environment creates a minor initiation that awakens one to that realm.

It is notable that virtually all formal Christian worship, except the Quaker meeting, uses music as an integral part of the service. The actual form used may vary widely: in Africa tribal drums may be employed; Benedictine monasteries may use the otherworldly strains of Gregorian chant; and in some Protestant churches "old time" gospel songs prevail. But in all cases, the power of music elevates and initiates the feelings into the sacred world of the inner planes.

A religious service often provides as much a link to the past of a culture or an individual as it provides a step into the sacred. Its art, its gestures, and its music as well as its message remind us of our individual history and no less of a larger past. Most religions tend to idealize earlier times as more religious than the present, whether (in the case of Christianity) in terms of the Catholic Middle Ages or the Protestant "old time religion" of the American frontier. Many parts of worship are actually constructed to bring back those days.

Christian worship is structured like a sacred perpetuation of New Testament times: of the life, death, and resurrection of Jesus Christ; of the coming of the Holy Spirit on Pentecost; and of the life of the early church. Symbolically, the Cross reminds us of the great events at the end of Jesus' earthly life, while the bread and wine of the Eucharist epitomize the Last Supper. In fact, this sacred ceremony is what all meals should ideally be: eating together in peace and harmony with God, with past and present, with friends and enemies, and with all things visible and invisible. The Eucharist brings us into harmony not only with the Last Supper but with the entire progression of the Christian faith. It reminds us of the great cathedrals and simple country churches, of Camelot and Christian soldiers, of missionaries and pilgrims in a hundred lands. The Eucharist also reminds us of the Grail, as the Grail reminds us of the Eucharist—both being half-hidden mysteries full of light and the power of regeneration, requiring faith and asking a question rather than giving an answer. For the bread and the wine, like the Cross, ask us whom they serve, and the correct answer is not given only in words.

Christianity offers powerful and joyous reminders of the past and symbols in the present through its great festivals. Nearly all Christians celebrate Christmas and Easter, times when the festive cup may be raised like the mythic Grail in halls of light and healing. In the seasons of preparation of Advent and Lent, self-denial is practiced. Some Christians also observe the feast of the Ascension of Christ, and then Whitsunday or Pentecost fifty days after Easter to commemorate the coming of the Holy Spirit to the disciples in the form of tongues of fire and a rushing mighty wind. And there are other holy days for various saints and sacred events, ranging from the Annunciation, in remembrance of the Archangel Gabriel's announcement to the Virgin Mary that she would become the mother of Our Lord, to the festival of her Assumption into heaven.

The Christian year with its festivals is part of the cycle through which the eternal is expressed in time. On the occasion of these festivals, time pauses for a moment, and the true nature of that which is beyond time can be revealed to us. A festival is a time of true community, when ordinary rules do not apply and people encounter each other's true humanity.

The Christmas festival recalls not only events of some two thousand years ago, when the Word became flesh and dwelt among us, but also the timeless time of the Beginning, when in the second great Outpouring the eternal Word gives form to all things. It reveals that creation is an ongoing process and not a finished deed. Moreover, it reminds us that the Word still becomes flesh moment by moment within our own hearts, if we allow Christ to be born as the light of our consciousness, giving wisdom, joy, unity of mind, and peace.

In the Easter festival, the black-veiled occurrences of Holy Week culminate in Good Friday and the joy beyond belief of Easter morning. This procession of events reminds us of the eternal crucifixion of spirit on the Cross of matter and the power of spirit to transform that matter from within. Then, at the Ascension, the new life of matter that has been transformed on all planes returns to heaven, symbolizing the recovered unity of all that is beyond time and space, the ultimate unity of body, mind, and spirit. When we are totally unified on all planes with no obstruction of the divine within, and the atma is visible, with all channels to it clear, we can be a mighty conduit of the divine energy streaming forth into the world. That is what Jesus became. This process began in his ministry of healing and miracles and culminated in the sacrament of the Last Supper that became the Eucharist, the ceremonial meal that many Christians believe still is a conduit for the divine grace that is in Jesus. His triumph on the Cross completed the work of unifying and opening that let this grace flow earthward in full abundance.

The first visible display of the new grace present in the world after Good Friday is the coming of the Holy Spirit on Pentecost. Descending upon the disciples in the upper room, the Holy Spirit made those men, who were at first so fearful and full of doubt, into apostles, the bold envoys of grace who began the great work of carrying the good news to the ends of the earth. As we celebrate Pentecost, we remember the Outpouring of the Holy Spirit at the beginning, the movement of wisdom and power that is now an eternal benediction that we can receive whenever our hearts yearn for it.

Finally, the great rites of formal initiation are also an important part of Christian life. There are several types that correlate to the "programmatic" and "natural" initiations mentioned previously. In most traditions, baptism with water is the common ritual of Christian initiation. Like crucifixion on the Cross of matter, baptism clearly symbolizes death and re-birth. Here, though, the symbol is water, which is matter's most primordial and chaotic form, the "deep" over which the Spirit brooded at the first creation. Coming out of these waters with a new name and new life in Christ signifies a personal resurrection. Baptism may be followed by confirmation, in which one receives the Holy Spirit in one's personalized Pentecost. Those who receive the calling may seek ordination to certain forms of ministry in the offices of deacon, priest, presbyter, or bishop, which is also reception of the Holy Spirit. These persons should be seen not as churchly lords, but as servants of the church body corporate—"servants of the servants of God." Their role is to help others live a better Christian life through their teaching, counsel, and transmission of grace by means of the church's public and private ministrations.

Initiations pertaining to life events include weddings, funerals, and sometimes such practices as anointing or laying-on-of-hands for the sick. The initiations of marriage, sickness, and death that life brings us can be profoundly transformative. It is natural, therefore, that the church has incorporated blessings and rituals which show that life's transitions have eternal as well as temporal meaning. For example, the marriage rite illustrates that the love binding a good marriage is the same love that exists between Christ and the church and between God and the world—the love that binds all things.

At the hour of death, Christians traditionally receive three things: anointing, absolution for forgiveness of sins, and Holy Communion. Death is perhaps the greatest crucifixion on the Cross of matter that we will receive on our journey. In that moment it seems as though matter is triumphant and that life itself has proved to be ephemeral. Yet that last Holy Communion is called the *viaticum* or "aid for the road," reminding us that in Christian and esoteric perception the last event is actually the beginning of another journey. And even though the road is unknown, we do not make this journey alone, for the presence of prayer and sacrament tells us that the whole company of the faithful—the communion of saints here and beyond—are our traveling companions.

Esoteric Christians honor the churches and temples of all faiths, since they recognize that in some manner all are hostels for pilgrims on the great Path. They also recognize the importance of corporate worship for the development of Christian love and charity, for receiving grace and the Holy Spirit, for the sake of good Christian deeds, and for the witness of those on this path. Thus, esoteric Christians ordinarily participate in public worship services weekly with whatever body of faithful they feel drawn toward, or they make private devotions that unite them spiritually with all others who worship. Because of its alignment with the spirit of medieval tradition and romance, and the great joy that underlies Christianity centered on the joy of the resurrection, Christian esotericists celebrate the joyous affirmation of festivals, including Christmas and Easter and perhaps Thanksgiving, Pentecost, the Ascension, the Assumption of the Blessed Virgin Mary, and All Saints Day after Halloween eve.

There are many paths within the Path. Christians may occasionally travel their path alone, but when they come together, it is occasion for celebration and joy. "Behold, how good and pleasant it is when brothers [and sisters] dwell in unity! For there the Lord has commanded the blessing, life for evermore" (Psalm 133). Life in the Christian community means life with other people just as we all are and in hope of what we shall be, before the end and the beginning of forever.

5

TWO OR THREE GATHERED TOGETHER: THE NATURE OF CHRISTIAN COMMUNITY

Christians, like any other group of people, are very ordinary and imperfect. Whether in church or prayer group—or even monastery, convent, or house of bishops—and regardless of denomination, Christians are mere human beings who can be sick, cantankerous, petty, and temperamental but then sometimes amazingly understanding and loving. The church and human society in general are really "mixed bags," capable of a wide range of moods, attitudes, and actions. We may glibly say, "Nobody's perfect," especially when that sentiment conveniently excuses our own lapses. We hasten to direct attention to the faults of others and even to divide the world into saints and sinners: "Christians versus unbelievers," or some other social, political, economic, racial, or nationalistic categorization of "good guys versus bad guys." But in reality there is good and evil on both sides of these divides and indeed within each person on each side—including ourselves. It thus makes sense to think of the church as a hospital for sinners, not a museum of saints.

On the other hand, it would be folly not to recognize that some people, causes, and actions are closer to the love at the heart of the universe than others. Activities based on hatred or greed are clearly more responsible for large-scale evil than those founded on the pure sentiments of compassion and peace. The real point is simply that all of us need as much help as we can get, and must, in the words of Jesus' parable, be slow to point out the splinter in someone else's eye while ignoring the beam in our own. There is virtually no one in whom God does not have something of value with which to work. The role of the church in this regard is to be a *schola caritatis*, or "school of charity and love," rather than a court of judgment. And herein is a great mystery. In the world as it is, the church is a training ground in love precisely because it is composed of highly imperfect persons: it is easy to love those who are already perfect, but the real test and training comes in loving the unlovable and bearing with the unbearable.

Esoteric Christianity is a way of initiation, and favoring the ill-favored is an initiatory ordeal, just like the test passed by the princess when she kissed the frog or by Beauty when she embraced the beast. Undergoing this initiation expands our hearts and vision and allows us to see God in new places. It is a triumph over self. In this school of love, the church is guru and classroom.

CHURCH AS COMMUNITY

How does the church foster an initiatory environment? First, those we encounter in the setting of
the church and its work in the world provide far more
than opportunities for charity alone. They are also
occasions when we can genuinely experience participation in another's life through mutual sharing and
learning. This happens in practical ways, such as confessing our faults to each other (James 5:16) or group
counseling in a community of trust. It is a great com-
fort to have a place where we can feel free to unbur-
den ourselves of things in our consciousness that
separate the divine within from that without. We
should first deal with personal shortcomings alone
in private prayers of honesty and confession. But we
are meant to be social beings, too, and we are not
entirely complete unless we share our burdens with
others in the church and in society. Symbols of mem-
bership in a group are often important to us. Recog-
nizing these needs, some churches make available
confession to a priest who gives counsel and absolution, and may even encourage public confession of
sins before the congregation. The church thus has
an opportunity to respond with love, forgiveness, and
support in the penitent's renewed life.

The forgiveness of sins is an essential part of
the esoteric work of the church. Others who are truly
motivated by love and understanding can be of immense help to us as we try to understand and love
ourselves despite our faults. A group in which we
are free to talk and even weep about our troubles

and then receive healing love is truly a household of God. In esoteric language, it is a place of initiation, for the very essence of initiation is the painful shedding of one life and being born to another, as the butterfly emerges from the cocoon.

To truly participate in communal esoteric initiation, you need to be willing to take on both roles: First, you must be willing to share your faults and say, "I've done something that's been on my mind. I think I was wrong, and I'd like get it off my chest. What can I do to make up for it with the person, with God, and with the universe?" Second, and when others speak similarly to you, you need to be open and serious without being condemnatory. Offer a moment's silent prayer or meditation and then say to the person, not what *you* think, but what comes through you.

Remember also to share the joys, good deeds, and virtues of others along with their sins and sorrows. The Buddhists, along with unlimited compassion (which literally means "suffering with"), have a wonderful complementary virtue: unlimited sympathetic joy. Surely it is important and a mark of true love of one's fellows to be able to share the joys of another being as deeply as the pain. Both are what oneness, a total interdependent relatedness, are about.

This sense of community is what the church should be and what it is about on a deep level—that of its worship and sacraments—whether it always realizes it or not. By the same token, any group of people—friends, coworkers, even those met only by accident or unexpected karma—that shares one another's sins, pain, and joy, *is* the church, at least for that moment. May such meetings happen often.

THE VALUE OF HIERARCHY IN RELIGION

We can also grow in love and initiation through participation in the organizational life of the church. This statement may seem facetious to some people. It is common in religious circles to make light of the functionaries who manage the institutional side of religion or to speak bitterly of the petty politics and bureaucratic jobbery that seems to overshadow parish offices and denominational headquarters. Yet in organized religion, as in all things, there is a hidden as well as an outer side, and there are opportunities for growth even in the most troubling situations. The traditional church has a vital role in manifesting structurally and symbolically what the ideal community ought to be. However unworthy in practice, it is a sacrament and sign of true fellowship.

Structure or hierarchy in human society, and above all in religion, can have several important purposes. First, it can teach us that it does not really exist. If Christian religion teaches us anything, it is that all souls are of infinite value and so are equal. The outer roles we enact are not the real person we are inside—not the real pilgrim beneath the roles—and may differ greatly from year to year and lifetime to lifetime. Roles often involve different "dress" for different parts, for clothing is often how society distinguishes between people who are nevertheless not so very different beneath their garbs of king and peasant, soldier and monk. A garment designating a person's role in the world, however, does identify that person as an envoy or agent of another power, and that is its point. The roles we assume can have the important spiritual function of leading us, first to appreciate the colorful diversity of human life, and then to look behind the roles to see that the hierarchy they imply is actually unreal. We soon learn that the people wearing those fascinating robes are all just human, as we are; they—as we—are all merely pilgrims on the Path, even though all are not necessarily at the same part of it. On this Path, the man in splendid archbishop's vestments may actually be well behind the woman in rags. Both roles have their place, and all are God in disguise.

Hierarchy or rank can remind us that we at once are both interdependent and have our own specialized tasks, even as different cells or organs in the body function. We need others as others need us. This is particularly true in religion, which teaches us that we need, not only the ultimate, but also our neighbor and one another. The two great commandments are to love God and to love your neighbor as yourself.

Moreover, organized religion can give us opportunities, as we bear with the faults of others, to love and return good for evil. It can help us learn when it is an act of love to admonish another person and when it is better to keep silent. As already mentioned, it can also provide contexts for the mutual confessing of sins and sharing of joys and pains.

Understanding our own role in the hierarchy can give us humility, and knowing when to be humble before the Wisdom that has assigned us a task is a good virtue to acquire along the way. The courage to manifest divine love must not come from the ego and its pride, but from the deepest possible sense of the interconnectedness of all things.

THE WEB OF LIFE

To explore and understand the role of hierarchy in the interrelated universe, begin with something small. A verse in Proverbs tells us that the spider can be held in the hand, yet it dwells in kings' palaces (Prov. 30:28).[1] That which seems small and insignificant can also be a part of something splendid. That is especially true in the case of the spider, for that tiny arachnid can spin a web extending for many feet, becoming most intricate and involved. Such a fine silvery web stretches out from each of us, too, growing out of our ultimate monadic nature to meet and interact with the webs of others, sensing the winds of the universe on all planes. It captures, it connects, it communicates, it reflects the light, and it deepens the shadows. The image of the web suggests the variety of our relations with ourselves and with all that is around us; it can also help us understand our relationships with God, grace, and the church—a seeming web of interrelatedness.

Exploring that web of life starts with the Holy Spirit. The Spirit is called by the Nicene Creed "the Lord, the Giver of Life." Life always begins its work

109

invisibly, from within. Flowers unfold from the secret interior of the bud and cannot be forced open without being destroyed; human life grows in the secret place of the womb until the time for birth. All through our life, growth of body or mind commences in the dark inwardness of flesh or consciousness, and only its consequences are seen. The Holy Spirit, "Lord and Giver of Life,"reigns within us in such a way that we do not even know we are being ruled, but say, "We did this ourselves."

EVOLUTION AND LOVE

The Holy Spirit is also the Lord of Love, for love, or compassion, the supreme virtue in Christianity— as in other religions—is the highest goal and fulfillment of life. Life is the interconnection of complex sets of elements and sub-systems into a harmonious, smoothly functioning greater system: the organism. Evolution, guided both from within and from the magnetism of its ultimate goal by the Holy Spirit, is the unimaginably vast process of such systems moving from relatively simple forms to the more complex: from the organic molecule to the one-celled creature to the plant; or from protozoa through fish and reptile and mammal to human. The process entails not only the increasing biological complexity of organisms, but also the union of consciousness and matter in intricate ways and the arrangement of organisms in systems larger than themselves: the herd, the family, the community, the nation, the world, the universe.

None of this necessarily occurs with ease. Physically, one part of an organism may not work in complete harmony with another: there may be deformities, distortions, too much of one secretion and not enough of another, even cancers. Serious impediments can occur between consciousness and the physical body, if what the mind decides it wants is not at all good for the body. And these problems may be compounded by the conflicts that can occur between an organism and its society: disharmony in the family, anger in the community, insurrection in the state, or violence between a group and the environment that is supposed to sustain it.

Yet life clearly desires evolution. Life's ruler and giver, the Holy Spirit, wants the systems to be working smoothly. An organism functions best when all its parts support each other and when mind and body are in harmony. Yet such harmony cannot be taken for granted, since on all levels the negative powers—disease, sin, will, destructive anger—can disrupt the flow.

The sublime expression of life as a harmonious system can be thought of as love. But love cannot be forced; it must come out of the freedom of an entity to harmonize with a larger system in a new and powerful relationship. That relationship is sustained by the appropriate emotional feeling, which is another way of saying that there is harmony between the self, the emotional plane, and the larger relationship. Love for self in the best sense, then, is harmony between mind, body, feelings, and social or natural environment. Love for others in particular is a preparation for harmoniously establishing the family as the system next larger than self. Love for others in general, and for community, nation, and world, creates symphonic harmonies rather than discordant dependencies within those larger spheres.

Love, then, is the expression of harmony for the benefit of life within increasingly complex systems and so must reflect unity in diversity and arise from freedom. On the deep level where all seeming differences find what they have in common, love is oneness. What blocks life is always that which separates—one organ working in disharmony with another, one organism fighting another, one thought or feeling disregarding another. Disease separates, anger and fear separate, preoccupation with self-identity separates. But love is the power within life that heals disunity by dissipating anger or fear and by revealing that there is nothing to be afraid of in acknowledging our interdependence with others. The supreme imperative is always love or compassion: putting the good of the other ahead of oneself, harmlessness to all beings, and affirming in word and deed the deep equality of all humans, and indeed of all beings.

The pilgrim lifestyle of a companion of the Cross and the Grail means above all affirming oneness with feeling and in practice. To this end, the church can be both a school and a means. The role of the church should be as a catalyst for unity, promoting oneness whether or not it gets credit, so busy loving the world that it does not care about itself. The Theosophical Society has as one of its objectives to be a nucleus of human brotherhood, which is another helpful image for the church. A nucleus is not the whole of anything, but rather is the center around which the whole positions itself and which even makes the whole possible. For example, the nucleus of a cell is not the whole cell, but it is essential to its life because it contains the genetic code that controls its development and metabolism.

All of this suggests appropriate ways for the church to work for the increase of love and harmony on the inner and outer levels and for the corresponding evolution of the planet through larger harmonious systems. The church may be thought of as an esoteric carrier of the genetic code for the harmonious future development of the world because of its particular relationship to the manifestation of the Christ-idea in Jesus. It can serve as a model for the life of the future. However, we should not think of it as the only bearer of those codes.

Too often the church appears to be a divisive and unhelpful part of society rather than a catalyst or nucleus for its betterment. If it persists in sometimes hindering evolution, it will undoubtedly be discarded, and the evolutionary process—we might even say, the Holy Spirit—will find other catalysts and nuclei. Just as Jesus was not the only Master of Wisdom, so Christianity and the Christian church are not the only spiritual/social forces within the world through which the Holy Spirit can work for evolution and the ultimate triumph of love, freedom, and oneness in diversity.

Our Role as Church Members

As members of the church, we need to understand and define for ourselves the role we can play
in evolution. What is it that we as members of the
Christian church, and particularly as esoteric Christians, have to offer the evolutionary task that others
of good will—political reformers, social workers, hu-
manists, visionaries in advance of their times—do not
have? Certainly it is not that we have any particular
clarity not given to others about how to make the
world a better place on the practical level. It is not
necessarily even that we have a greater degree of sincerity or dedication based on deep love and compassion for our fellow beings than do those less religious
than we.

Instead, it is something of an entirely different
order. Traditional religion puts all that we do in a far
larger context than does any other perspective. It is
the perspective which considers not only the visible
world, but also the invisible: the world of spirits,
gods, angels, and saints. It is a view not only of a
living planet stuck in an inert universe, but also of
the deep background out of which we came as children of Heaven and Earth; of the parental background of matter and consciousness; and of our ultimate environment—infinite reality itself. Esoteric
Christianity draws and correlates ways of understanding the ultimate background both from traditional
Christianity, with its saints and angels and kingdom
of heaven, and from the esoteric tradition, which com-
prehends such entities through concepts like the in-

ner planes. If the esoteric tradition is articulated through the Theosophical tradition, the opening line of C.W. Leadbeater's little book *Invisible Helpers* seems relevant: "It is one of the most beautiful characteristics of Theosophy that it gives back to people in a more rational form everything which was really useful and helpful to them in the religions which they have outgrown."[2]

Some would not say, however, that they have outgrown other forms of religion. Others may feel that, although they find much in the traditional forms of religion hard to believe, at the same time they cannot avoid a sense that the universe is deeper and more wondrous—and more alive—than it appears on the surface. Science, of course, works on that surface. Much scientific knowledge is magnificent both for its useful technological applications and for the awesome universe of subatomic particles and billions of galaxies it has unveiled, together with the profound understanding it has given us of the functioning of life and mind. Yet understanding how things really *are* on the planes beneath what can be viewed and *why* they are what they are remains for other languages or for that which can be spoken only through silence. For in the final evolutionary thrust toward the fulfillment of life in love and of oneness through diversity, we need to bring together inner and outer, speech and silence, things spoken and unspoken, all things visible and invisible.

The fellowship of the church ought to be helpful here. This fellowship, however, must include all beings on all planes entitled to our love and fellowship—it must include all that is. We need to let the web of our individual lives intertwine with those of others in the church and then both individually and corporately send out filaments of feeling and sympathy onto many levels. We are obligated in joy to help those around us on the same plane of existence as ourselves: the unloved, the sorrowing, and the angry, those consumed with guilt and those in need; the poor, the homeless, the sick, and those who are in prison; and no less those of the animal world who hunger and thirst, who are abused and enslaved, who are raised miserably only to be slaughtered amid blood and fear.

On our plane we also find help: eyes that are wise, voices unwavering for right amid the evils of the world, and, above all, fellowship of those who, however imperfect themselves, know that in gathering together we find strength. What we as a church corporate do together makes avenues of power through which divine energies can flow. In these challenges and strengths lies the active church here on this visible earth.

The church and its people must also reach out to those who are *not* visible, and herein lies its uniqueness: It can minister to those on the astral plane who need help in releasing themselves from suffering. It can also realize the meaning of the fellowship of saints and angels by knowing how to reach out to the compassionate love and power of these high and holy ones on the other side. These are beings who, in Theosophical terms, are on the mental plane for the most part, though a few work on the astral plane out of compassion and for the opportunities it affords; for the same reason, some are also in this world in physical form, whether known or unknown. They can respond to us when we reach out to them, and they are able to support us, work with us, touch our innermost thoughts, and even help us rise above our karma.

All of this, then, is what the fellowship of the church ought to include. In your own way, in your own life, in your own church, make your fellowship as large as you possibly can. Expand your mind and heart and inner awareness to those in need and to those who can help on all planes, not forgetting to use the channels that can be opened by prayer, sacrament, and thought-forms. This practice allows the power of invisible friends and helpers to radiate through to this world and also allows our help and thoughts to go out to them. Thus, the visible church can mystically serve as a model of the complexity and interrelatedness of the world visible and invisible.

6

A LITTLE CHILD: CHRISTIAN ETHICS

esus said, "Whosoever shall not receive the kingdom of heaven as a little child, shall not enter therein" (Matt. 18:3); "Take heed that ye despise not one of these little ones" (Matt. 18:10); "Inasmuch as ye have done it unto one of the least of these my brethren, ye have done it unto me" (Matt. 25:40); and "Unless you turn and become like children, you will never enter the kingdom of heaven. Whoever humbles himself like this child, he is the greatest in the kingdom of heaven" (Matt. 18:3-4).

In some deep sense the child, fresh and marvelous, is at the center of all esoteric Christianity, the most romantic of all religions. A childlike sense of wonder is the key to understanding the mysteries of the esoteric universe.

How children are regarded is the ultimate test of any personal, community, or political ethics. The child, for Jesus, was the ultimate test. Nothing in the adult intellectual, political, or economic world had any value to him if it caused a single child to suffer or do wrong: "Whoever causes one of these little ones who believe in me to sin, it would be better for him to have a great millstone fastened round

his neck and to be drowned in the depth of the sea"
(Matt. 18:6). Children are emblematic of the defenseless—the poor, the lame, and those of despised
and outcast races, genders, and classes. Protecting
and helping a child, even if the child is not one's own,
is a supreme and sublime act of selfless love. It is
esoterically another great initiatory test, answering
in deed if not in word the mysterious question of the
quest: "Whom does the Grail serve?"

The child at the center of Christian ethics can
reveal a hidden dualism between individual and social ethics. In the Gospel, Jesus tells Christians that
they must do the following in order to receive eternal life:

> A certain teacher of the Law came up and
> tried to trap Jesus. Master, he asked, what must
> I do to receive eternal life? Jesus answered him,
> What do the Scriptures say? How do you inter-
> pret them? The man answered, You must love
> the Lord your God with all your heart, and with
> all your soul, and with all your strength, and
> with all your mind; and, You must love your
> neighbor as yourself. Your answer is correct,
> replied Jesus, do this and you will live. (Luke
> 10:25-28)

Jesus says nothing here about belief in himself
as being important in order for us to receive eternal
life. Instead, love of God and love of neighbor appear to be the necessary criteria, and Jesus gives us
the parable of the Good Samaritan to explain just

who our neighbor is:

> But the teacher of the Law wanted to put himself in the right, so he asked Jesus, Who is my neighbor? Jesus answered, A certain man was going down from Jerusalem to Jericho, when robbers attacked him, stripped him and beat him up, leaving him half dead. It so happened that a priest was going down that road; when he saw the man he walked by on the other side. In the same way, a Levite also came there, went over and looked at the man, and then walked by on the other side. But a certain Samaritan who was traveling that way came upon him, and when he saw the man his heart was filled with pity. He poured oil and wine on his wounds and bandaged them; then he put the man on his own animal and took him to an inn, where he took care of him. The next day he took out two silver coins and gave them to the innkeeper. Take care of him, he told the innkeeper, and when I come back this way I will pay you back whatever you spend on him. And Jesus concluded, Which one of these three seems to you to have been a neighbor to the man attacked by the robbers? The teacher of the Law answered, The one who was kind to him. Jesus replied, Go then and do likewise. (Luke 10:29-37)

St. John in his first epistle states bluntly that love for others—the neighbor, the child, the defenseless—

is the one and only test of sincerity in any claims of love for God:

> If someone says, "I love God," yet hates his brother, he is a liar. For he cannot love God, whom he has not seen, if he does not love his brother, whom he has seen. This, then, is the command that Christ gave us: he who loves God must love his brother also. (I John 4:20-21)

Jesus insisted that love of neighbor means actual involvement—sacrificing time and energy and taking direct action to help those who are in need. He also said that such direct action is the one great test, the one initiatory ordeal, of our belief in Christ and love for him:

> When the Son of Man comes as king, and all the angels with him, he will sit on his royal throne, and all the earth's people will be gathered before him. Then he will divide them into two groups, just as a shepherd separates the sheep from the goats: he will put the sheep at his right and the goats at his left. Then the king will say to the people on his right: You who are blessed by my Father come! Come and receive the kingdom which has been prepared for you since the creation of the world. I was hungry and you fed me, thirsty and you gave me drink; I was a stranger and you received me in your homes, naked and you clothed me; I was sick and you took care of me, in prison and you

visited me. The righteous will then answer him: When, Lord, did we ever see you hungry and feed you, or thirsty and give you drink? When did we ever see you a stranger and welcome you in our homes, or naked and clothe you? When did we ever see you sick or in prison and visit you? The king will reply, I tell you, indeed, whenever you did this for one of the least important of these brothers of mine, you did it for me! (Matt. 25:31-40)

Loving the neighbor, binding wounds, feeding the hungry, giving drink to the thirsty, receiving the stranger into our home, clothing the naked, caring for the sick, visiting those in prison, caring for the child: these are imperatives addressed to all of us.

Today, we argue about whether charity or welfare should be dispensed by government, churches, private agencies, or individuals acting on their own. The prophets and Jesus, perhaps not expecting too much from the ruthless rulers of their times, left this question open. But Christian kings such as Arthur did not neglect compassion for the poor and helpless. The hungry child, after all, does not care *where* the bread and milk comes from—whether it be the state, the church, or the Red Cross. Surely these are the feelings of God, or of his son Jesus, when he appears to us in the pale mask of one who is hungry and thirsty.

The expectation is that we will respond in a way appropriate to our means and that we will not only bind up the wounds of victims of the world's evils but also attack the sources of those evils. St. Paul tells us that the reason we pay taxes is so that we can support the authorities who are "ministers of God" and whose obligation it is to punish evildoers (Rom. 13:6, 4).

Selfless giving is the essence of chivalry, that code of the medieval knights who served King Arthur and the Grail and who are our ideal in the romantic and esoteric side of Christianity. As embodiments of chivalry, esoteric Christians are expected to always serve the poor, protect the weak, and labor for justice among persons and nations. The faith allows no discrimination or injustice among its members or in society on the basis of creed, race, gender, sexual orientation, relative wealth or poverty, education or lack thereof.

To fulfill this ideal, every Christian should have an ongoing commitment to the important labor of unpaid, volunteer work and should try to be a peacemaker whenever possible. Esoteric Christians regard the accounts of armed conflict in the Bible and the Grail legends as essentially allegorical; thus, honoring the Sermon on the Mount, they stress the power of nonviolence and the chivalrous courage that the practice of its teachings requires. However, forceful means may nonetheless sometimes be required, and the issue of vocation to the police or military professions must be left to individual conscience.

In answer to the question, "What is the function of orderly knighthood?" the twelfth-century English philosopher John of Salisbury wrote:

To protect the Church, to fight against treachery, to reverence the priesthood, to fend off injustice from the poor, to make peace in your own province, to shed blood for your brethren, and if needs must, to lay down your life.[1]

Esoteric Christians may consider whatever commitment they make to protect Christ's creatures in terms of such a chivalric vow. We could modernize John of Salisbury's words this way:

I vow to protect all spiritual paths; to fight against treachery; to reverence all custodians of learning, culture, and spirituality; to fend off injustice to the poor; to work for peace in my own home, neighborhood, and land; to defend all my human sisters and brothers, by nonviolent means insofar as I am able; and, if necessary to that end, to lay down my life.

CHRISTIAN ETHICAL OBLIGATIONS

Clearly the care of the poor and defenseless— and of the child at the center—is a primary biblical and Christian ethical obligation. Yet many other decisions about right and wrong face us almost every day of our lives: how to deal kindly and honestly with a difficult situation at home or work; issues of whether a certain business practice or political commitment is ethical; and the weighty matters of sexual or medical ethics. What kind of sexual relationships are really proper? When is marital separation, annulment, or divorce the right course of action? How hard do you try to hold a marriage together? When, if ever, is abortion acceptable? What about euthanasia or mercy killing for the terminally ill? Is suicide ever justified? Are animal experiments?

Ethicists tell us there are basically two ways religious or philosophical ethical decisions are made. One, technically called the deontological, is derived from what is perceived to be the will of God or the nature of being: divine command, natural law, the mode of behavior that is clearly built into the nature of things. People working from this starting point would argue that the Ten Commandments are the revealed will of God, and so we must honor our parents and not kill or commit adultery or bear false witness just because God commands it. They would also say that, since sexual organs were obviously made for the purpose of procreation, it is contrary to natural law to use them in other ways. They might contend—along with certain Hindus—that the division of society into castes with different tasks and different degrees of purity is an aspect of the eternal order of things.

The other approach, technically called the teleological or consequentialist, starts from the opposite end, or from the results of an action. Does the action actually result in what we would consider human or social good? Obviously, before making such a judgment, we need to have a clear idea of what we consider good for individual humans or for society as a whole. But the consequentialist perspective does allow for some flexibility, if that is itself regarded as good. Would a certain amount of killing, as in war, result in greater good in the end? Would sexual expression even when procreation is not intended strengthen marital love and human good? These are the kinds of questions addressed by teleology.

Most Christians, like most people in general, make ethical decisions based upon an informal combination of both these approaches. Jesus himself did as much, for he told the young teacher of the Law to keep the commandments, yet he also said, "By their fruits ye shall know them," and taught the rule of love as supreme. Love itself seems to entail ethical flexibility, for in each instance we must assess the overall situation and the personalities concerned regarding whether we need to admonish (as Jesus did the "hypocrites" who kept the letter but not the spirit of the Law) or to forgive (as Jesus did the adulterous woman). In other words, love means following not the moral letter of the law but whatever will best facilitate the inward evolution toward the Light of those who will receive the consequences of the ethical decision: the spouse, the patient, the victim, or the victor.

This is a tricky matter, since our sight and insight are so often clouded by our own passions, ignorance, and sheer mental limitations. In most cases, however, it is far better to follow conventional morality, which at least has the wisdom of the ages behind it, than to follow a path in which our own passions or wishful thinking may fool us about the true nature of love. We should usually perceive danger if the proposed action specifically contravenes the Ten

Commandments or other conventional morality. Yet love is the supreme law and the supreme road back to the Light. The esoteric tradition can help us realize this truth within the Christian framework.

The esoteric and Theosophical traditions, like Buddhism and Vedanta, maintain the profundity of oneness—the interrelatedness of the universe behind all apparent separation. This concept is a basis for both deontological and consequentialist ethics. Its first principle is that the most ethical action comes out of a deep realization of unity—of humans with nature, of individuals and society—and that this realization is no different than a profound grasp of universal love. Its second principle is that the only means by which an action can finally be judged is whether it enhances and increases love in the world. You and I, oneness whispers, are a part of all we meet, and what we do to others we do to ourselves, for "Inasmuch as ye have done it unto the least of these my brethren, ye have done it unto me" —and the Christ who said this is in the deepest sense *none other than our own true nature!* For we live in Christ, and he in us.

Contemporary scholars have emphasized the commensality that was central to Jesus' ministry; that is, his willingness to sit down and eat with virtually anyone. It is a significant message that despite criticism Jesus ate with high and low, clean and unclean, publicans and prostitutes alike. This sort of commensality is a concrete, practical expression of oneness. It is a recognition that we are all the same, all divine beneath the surface. Yet many who talk easily about mystical oneness would find it exceedingly hard to actually sit and eat with the homeless, the dirty and smelly, the poor or the mentally disturbed, or even with people of a different race or nation! But Jesus demonstrated by his actions that thinking is of little worth without doing. For us too, then, love and life in Christ entails the obligation of eating together. Commensality is the sublime sign by which Jesus broke down social barriers between the prince and the pauper. He accepted a place at all tables and offered his table to all, even as, mirroring Christ's virtues, Arthur's Round Table was open to all who demonstrated inner nobility.

The child at the center, who is the key to all personal and social ethics, is out there in the world—whether at home or homeless on the streets, whether trying to play in a city dump or living lonely and unloved in a mansion. Ethical religion means looking out toward the other, as well as inward: "True religion and undefiled before God and the Father is this: to visit orphans and widows in their affliction, and to keep oneself unstained from the world" (James 1:27). But the child is also the unstained part of us within, which is our true nature toward God, the inner Christ whom we see as the child in the manger, on the Cross, and in the hungry and sick of all ages.

We may also see the child-nature in animals. It is no accident that children often have a special love for animals, for they undoubtedly see them as creatures like themselves: full of feelings, desires, and the capacity to love and be loved, yet utterly dependent on the mercy and care of guardians (or persecutors). This leads to another important issue.

CHRISTIANITY AND VEGETARIANISM

Eating animal flesh versus vegetarianism is certainly a matter of ethical concern. Though opinion and practice are by no means unanimous, both Eastern and Western spirituality contain traditions favoring vegetarianism as an expression of moral and spiritual sensitivity. The vegetarianism of the Jains and of many Hindus, Buddhists, and Taoists is well known. In the West, the exclusion of animal products from one's diet was taught by the ancient Pythagoreans, by certain austere medieval monastic orders, and by followers of nineteenth-century movements ranging from Seventh-Day Adventism to Theosophy. In the late twentieth century, vegetarianism is conspicuously gathering strength. Perhaps before two or three more centuries have passed, it will be the prevailing norm.[2]

Four powerful arguments can be made on behalf of vegetarianism as a diet and a way of life. First, in terms of health, studies show that vegetarians generally live longer and healthier lives than do meat eaters. Second, from an ecological perspective, we live in a world of rapidly expanding population and decreasing oceanic resources and land available for agriculture. It is important to remember that the same amount of land and water could and should support many more people on a healthy vegetarian diet than when it is devoted to meat production. Third, for humanitarian reasons, no one should eat

meat unless he or she has visited the revolting factory farms and slaughterhouses from which most of
it comes today and has seen the suffering there; few
people of any sensitivity who do so will want to eat
meat again. Fourth, from a spiritual viewpoint a vegetarian diet can give one a pure, peaceful feeling,
including a feeling of love for all creatures, that flows
naturally into good prayer and meditation. As the
Ancient Mariner said in Coleridge's poem, "He
prayeth best who loveth best/All things both great
and small."

But what about Christianity and vegetarianism?
Conventional Christianity has failed to come to terms
with the moral issues involved in the killing of animals for food. We can only hope that in time the spiritual evolution of the religion will lead it to do so. If
not, it is likely that the spirituality of the world at
large will pass it by.

Admittedly, the Christian religion has few
grounds in its history on which to oppose meat-eating. The Old Testament people ate meat, or dreamed
of eating meat, from the quails of the Exodus (Ex.
16:13-14; cf. Num. 11) to the sacrifices of the temple
with their butchering of terrified lambs and calves
and their whole burnt offerings of animal flesh. Jesus
ate fish and perhaps meat, and in the parable of the
prodigal son apparently commended the killing of
the fatted calf to celebrate the wayward boy's return.
St. Peter saw a vision of a sheet that was let down
from heaven full of creatures, clean and unclean, and
heard the divine words, "Rise, Peter, kill and eat"
(Acts 10:9-16). St. Paul refused to condemn, unless

for the sake of those weaker than he in the faith, eating meat offered to idols (I Cor. 8:7-9).

Yet there are other rich and profound biblical themes that appear to support vegetarianism. The book of Genesis seems to consider animal killing and meat-eating a consequence of the human fall into sin, for Adam and Eve did none of that in Eden before the coming of the serpent. Isaiah, in a powerful prophesy of the "peaceable kingdom," calls the final days a time of return to that blessed beginning when,

> The wolf shall live with the lamb,
> the leopard shall lie down with the kid,
> the calf and the lion and the fatling together,
> and a little child shall lead them.
> The cow and the bear shall graze,
> their young shall lie down together;
> and the lion shall eat straw like the ox.
> The nursing child shall play over the hole of the asp,
> and the weaned child shall put its hand in the adder's den.
> They will not hurt or destroy on all my holy mountain;
> for they will be full of the knowledge of the Lord as the waters cover the sea. (Isa. 11:6-9)

In the New Testament, the sacrifice of Christ on the Cross means once and for all the end of the bloody sacrifices of the old law:

For if the blood of goats and bulls, with sprin-
kling of the ashes of a heifer, sanctifies those
who have been defiled so that their flesh is pu-
rified, how much more will the blood of Christ,
who through the eternal Spirit offered himself
without blemish to God, purify our conscience
from dead works to worship the living God!
(Heb. 9:13-14). . . . And it is by God's will that
we have been sanctified through the offering
of the body of Jesus Christ once for all. (Heb.
10:10)

Within the meaning of this sacrifice, and in the
even greater meaning of the incarnation of God in
Christ that underlies it, is a still deeper mystery of
love that is only beginning to unfold in Christian consciousness. That is the mystery of the self-empty-
ing of God in Christ as the outpouring of the love of
the Greater on behalf of the lesser.[3]

Let the same mind be in you that was in Christ
Jesus
Who, though he was in the form of God,
did not regard equality with God
as something to be exploited,
but emptied himself,
taking the form of a slave
being born in human likeness.
And being found in human form, he humbled
himself
and became obedient to the point of death—
even death on a cross.

Therefore God also highly exalted him,
and gave him the name
that is above every name, so that at the name
of Jesus
every knee should bend,
in heaven and on earth and under the earth,
and every tongue should confess that Jesus
Christ is Lord,
to the glory of God the Father. (Phil. 2:6-11)

Here the cosmic Christ is humbling himself to become the plain and vulnerable man who let himself be hung on the Cross, as part of making known "the mystery that has been hidden throughout the ages and generations but has now been revealed to his saints" (Col. 1:26). This same Christ was especially manifested in Jesus as the second Outpouring of creation. According to the author of Colossians, "He is the image of the invisible God, the firstborn of all creation; for in him all things in heaven and on earth were created, things visible and invisible . . . for in him all the fullness of God was pleased to dwell" (Col. 1:15-19). And not only did Jesus, as the incarnation of the Christ, contain all things, but in his once-and-for-all sacrifice they were made right with God: "Through him God was pleased to reconcile to himself all things, whether on earth or in heaven, by making peace through the blood of his cross" (Col. 1:20).

This is where meat-eating and the ethical treatment of animals becomes critical. The inflicting of pain and terror on another creature is the opposite of reconciliation and the opposite of having the mind of Christ in us. Christ instead showed us the true greatness of power in the love of the Greater for the lesser, rather than in the exploitation of the lesser by the greater, as we do in the farmyard and the slaughterhouse. As Paul says, "the creation waits with eager longing for the revealing of the children of God" when "the creation will itself be set free from its bondage to decay and will obtain the freedom of the glory of the children of God," for "we know that the whole creation has been groaning in labor pains until now." (Rom. 8:19-22). Who suffers more than those animals raised, often in pitiful conditions, only for the butcher's knife? Surely they must be among the "all things" in creation with whom those who have the mind of Christ must make peace and live in peace.

The animal world, for all the mystery of suffering it undergoes, is part of the redeemed cosmos. If we are to dwell in Christ and he in us, our part is not to abuse or exploit but to protect and save those orders lesser than us, even as Christ saved us. Yet they are not truly lesser but, as St. Francis might have put it, brothers and sisters of other furs and faces, and humans have been given a special responsibility towards them. Genesis tells us that humans have been given dominion over the beasts:

> Then God said, "Let us make humankind in our image, according to our likeness; and let them have dominion over the fish of the sea, and over the birds of the air, and over the cattle,

and over all the wild animals of the earth, and over every creeping thing that creeps upon the earth."

So God created humankind in his image, in the image of God he created them; male and female he created them.

God blessed them, and God said to them, "Be fruitful and multiply, and fill the earth and subdue it; and have dominion over the fish of the sea and over the birds of the air and over every living thing that moves upon the earth." God said, "See, I have given you every plant yielding seed that is upon the face of all the earth, and every tree with seed in its fruit; you shall have them for food. And to every beast of the earth, and to every bird of the air, and to everything that creeps on the earth, everything that has the breath of life, I have given every green plant for food." And it was so. (Gen. 1:26-30)

Note that in this commission, given before the fall into sin, only plant food is mentioned. The dominion over animals according to Genesis clearly means guardianship, not exploitation or enslavement. In his unfallen state Adam named the animals (Gen. 2:19-20), and what one names one loves best. Surely Adam and Eve were, in relation to the animals, meant to be like God the Good Shepherd in another of Isaiah's wondrous visions:

He will feed his flock like a shepherd;

he will gather the lambs in his arms,
and carry them in his bosom,
and gently lead the mother sheep. (Isa. 40:11)

CHRIST AND THE STATE

Finally, we must ask what kind of political structures are indicated by Christian ethics. Certainly they cannot, and should not, be spelled out in full detail. To begin with, the sources are not specific. The New Testament writers do not appear to have ever imagined that their faith would be the dominant religion of a society, much less of many great nations.

In theory, Christian nations should establish laws and a political structure commensurate with the highest values of their faith. Of course, this has not happened. By and large, Christian nations have not been consistently and conspicuously more virtuous than others. Certainly one can point to developments in the Christian world in the nineteenth and twentieth centuries, such as the abolition of slavery and some social welfare legislation, that owe much to the efforts of reformers who were seriously motivated by Christian values. But there has also been much hypocrisy and worse in the history of Christianity as it has interacted with states and societies. One must conclude that the City of God, or the kingdom of heaven, like the Grail castle, has always been both in and out of this world, a glittering and tantalizing ideal, yet never quite grasped and held steady. How do we endure the tension of being in sight of the kingdom yet never able to live in it?

Reinhold Niebuhr, famous theologian of the Union Theological Seminary in New York, thought of himself as a Christian realist. He believed that sin is always with us as part of our human freedom. He held that *utopianism*, the belief that humans can create an ideal society without sin, would only lead to worse than what we have now. He thought that belief in an earthly kingdom of God established by ordinary historical and political processes would end in the idolatry of thinking that one nation, ideology, or religion should triumph over all others.[4] Actually, the best we can look for in the political realm is justice, not pure love. Justice can only be informed by love which truly cares about the good of others, including the helpless child and social outcasts. But the state must express this love justly, fairly, and equally, not with disproportionate generosity. Love can give freely, but justice imposes obligations.

Although Niebuhr was not an esotericist, his viewpoint has something in common with esotericism. Esoteric Christians also have to live with tensions between inner and outer realities, order and freedom, justice and love. We do not need to be as pessimistic as Niebuhr about the evolutionary destiny of the world, though we need to take seriously his belief that utopianism is likely to lead to disaster. The best we can do is work for reforms and improvements that express love through justice and are consistent with the ideals of the kingdom. As the barriers to thought and sight between inner and outer planes fall away, these tensions will fall away as well.

There are a number of political values that esoteric Christians must keep in balance. One is the affirmation of tradition. Tradition maintained with a heavy hand or by the force of law can be oppressive. However, any religion would be impoverished without the traditions that give it life and color and link us to something larger than ourselves. Rituals, festivals, music, and vestments keep alive pieces of the ancient wisdom and often have deeper meanings than those of which we are aware.

Likewise, esoteric Christians must favor freedoms consistent with a just and compassionate society. This is particularly true regarding freedom of religion, since this freedom is affected by many others, such as freedom of the press, the right to peaceful assembly, and private property ownership. Esoteric Christians must also remember that compassion means respecting the rights and feelings of others, even those with whom they may disagree.

Compassion has always been a pillar of any good society, along with tradition and freedom. Tradition and freedom can, at times, seem at odds with each other, while compassion is a mediating theme as well as an irreducible value in itself.

Compassion has other dimensions as well. In a just society, compassion must be expressed through justice, not "feel good" sentimentality. Artificial equality is, in fact, the opposite of justice. Some inequality in wealth and position is necessary and is a natural outcome of basic freedoms, such as the right to private property. Different people make different choices and have various priorities, and these factors will not always lead to exactly the same economic results. But real, practical opportunity must be equally available to all.

Beyond these basic values, esoteric Christianity proposes no particular form of social order. What matters is that the principle of equality is extended to all and that all citizens are granted an active role in the selection of their political leaders. This equality should also include the rights of citizens to due process of law and to the other freedoms previously discussed.

All of this, Jesus reminds us, is simply for the sake of the child, the little one who represents the kingdom of heaven. History's mighty procession of kings and presidents, congresses and parliaments, courts and armies has in the end no other purpose than to ensure that this little child gets love and daily bread.

7

A GREAT WHILE BEFORE DAWN: PRAYER, MEDITATION, AND SPIRITUAL LIFE

lthough devotion to the church and a good social order are important, the Christian is not likely to achieve much without something deep, private, and joyous inside. This is the place of prayer, meditation, and spirituality.

This kind of worship is not public but is done when we are at least inwardly alone. It is akin to the mystical experience of Moses on the mountain when he communed with God and then returned to the people, his face shining with the glow of the Divine (Exod. 33, 34). Similarly, we are told that Jesus rose before dawn "and went to a lonely place, and there he prayed" (Mark 1:35).

Scripture gives us at least three styles of prayer. First, there is formal prayer: "Evening, and morning, and at noon, will I pray, and cry aloud; and he shall hear my voice" (Ps. 55:17). Whether it is once a day in the morning, or three times a day, or seven times a day as in some monastic communities, formal prayer is practiced at set intervals and often with a set repertoire of praise, penitence, and petition.

Then there is meditation, the inward quieting

of the mortal mind so that the mind of God may speak. "Thou shalt meditate therein day and night" (Josh. 1:8); "Commune with your own heart upon your bed, and be still" (Ps. 4:4); "My heart was hot within me; while I was musing the fire burned" (Ps. 39:3). Stillness and fire, the dark watches of the night—these are among the mysteries of meditation, the adventure that happens when we let go of our ordinary mind and silently open ourselves to the Divine.

Lastly, there is perpetual prayer: "Pray without ceasing" (I Thess. 5:17); "O how I love thy law! It is my meditation all the day" (Ps. 119:97). Is it really possible to pray all the time or to be so closely united with God that even prayer is not quite the right word for that unceasing friendship? The saints asked this question repeatedly, and it has been the subject of several holy books, such as that classic of Russian Orthodoxy, *The Way of the Pilgrim*.[1] We shall refer to prayer without ceasing as "the practice of the presence."

Prayer, meditation, and the practice of the presence are each spiritual practices in their own right. It would be a mistake to view them as successive rungs on a spiritual ladder, as though one started with mere ordinary prayer, then graduated to meditation, and finally went to some sort of post-graduate work of practicing the presence of God without ceasing. All three devotions are important and necessary for a well-rounded spiritual life. Keep them together, each in its time and for its own purpose.

Prayer involves words, feelings, ideas, expression, and often emotion exchanged between ourselves and God. None of these are easy. Prayer requires utter honesty, and there are self-anointed saints out there, not to mention ordinary people, for whom honesty is not as easy as piety. Some who consider themselves to be spiritual would rather just quiet the mind in meditation or think pleasant thoughts of God than deal with the hard issues that are at the heart of prayer. Prayer is a struggle for honesty and expression. It is not for cowards or hypocrites, like the ones Jesus condemned when he spoke of those who "devour widows' houses, and for pretense make long prayers" (Mark 12:40). Rather, it is for those who hear these words: "When you pray, go into your room and shut the door and pray to your Father who is in secret; and your Father who sees in secret will reward you" (Matt. 6:6). Secret prayer to the secret God. . . .

It may be hard even to believe in the reality of prayer, especially for some esoteric Christians whose concept of God may be impersonal. The idea of a secret God may have some meaning for them, but what is that secret prayer like, and who hears it in secret?

Here's where hard, tough honesty begins. The way we think of God really mirrors the way we think of ourselves. If with the saints, you have transcended all thought of ego or separate selfhood and live only in universal love, then you can truly understand and pray to the God who is beyond the level of anthropomorphic personality. But if you still think of yourself as personal, then the God with whom you can and must relate, if you are going to relate at all, is the personal God that the mystics have seen as real and as the manifestation of the transcendent God as Creator and Lord of the world. This personal God is not a dream; this God is there for you. It is this God with whom you need to struggle in prayer and against whom you need to test your ego, if you are going to get anywhere spiritually.

How then do you pray? You may use set prayers and phrases like those provided in church or those words of the so-called Lord's Prayer, which Jesus taught his disciples:

> Our Father, Who art in heaven;
> Hallowed be thy Name.
> Thy Kingdom come,
> Thy will be done,
> On earth, as it is in heaven.
> Give us this day our daily bread
> And forgive us our sins,
> As we forgive those who sin against us.
> Lead us not into the way of temptation,
> But deliver us from evil.
> For thine is the kingdom, and the power, and the glory,
> For ever and ever. Amen. (Matt. 6:9-13)

Set prayers may sound like a lazy method, but there is more to the matter than that. They are expressions that are hallowed by centuries of use and have associated with them powerful thought-forms on the inner planes that make them avenues of ascending consciousness and descending grace. The use of such phrases helps to steady the activity of thought and to center one's attention on God. And the very use of words that are not your own but have been hallowed by Jesus, the saints, and the church may be seen as an act of humility that can smooth the edges of ego.

Therefore, if the set prayers say what you want to say, use them in your devotions. Some may wish to use a Breviary, an Orthodox prayer book, the *Book of Common Prayer*,[2] or the *Liturgy* of the Liberal Catholic Church.[3] Whatever form is used, it is recommended that it include a Scripture lesson, psalms, and perhaps a hymn. The prayers should include praise, penitence, petition for your own spiritual and material needs, and intercession for others and for the world.

If you prefer to devise your own format, it should include praise, confession, learning, psalms or poems, petition (prayer for self), intercession (prayer for others), and benediction.

Prayer does not stop here, however. You must also learn to pray from the heart and in your own words. Confess to God what is wrong with you as you are, and tell God what you need on the deepest levels. Set yourself before God as the source of your life and its ultimate center.

Don't be afraid to argue with God—Judaism and Christianity are the only religions in which one *can* argue with God about justice and destiny, as far as I know. We can argue with passionate hope, as Abraham argued about the fate of Sodom and

Gomorrah (Gen. 18:20-33); as Job laid before God his unjust suffering with tremendous honesty; and as Jesus prayed for reprieve in the garden of Gethsemane (Luke 22:39-46). Pray until there are no more words to be spoken and there is silence, and listen into the silence for the answer of God and his blessing. When prayer has become silence and blessing, it is time to meditate.

Meditation is a means of getting in touch with the consciousness of God. It is knowing God and knowing ourselves as we are behind the chaos of the active mind. Most of us will engage in both prayer and meditation. Prayer takes on the Cross of salvation, while meditation, once attained, is full of peace, beyond ordinary consciousness, opening up to the deep joy on the other side.

Before discussing how to meditate, we need to be clear on what meditation is. For our purposes, "meditation" refers to techniques for stilling the random thoughts of the conscious mind—the "monkey mind," as it is called in Zen, that is always jumping from one thought to another as a monkey jumps from branch to branch.

Meditation is the practice of disciplining the mind to focus on a single object, thought, or sound. It can involve concentrating on an image of religious value or on other focal points. Zen practitioners count the breaths or just follow the breath in "mindfulness of breathing." Yoga practitioners use postures and may visualize a symbol of the divine within, such as a star or point of light. Others use an outer visual focus such as a candle flame, an audial focus such as a mantra, or even something in nature—the sun, the moon, the sound of rain on the roof. It doesn't matter; the focal point doesn't need to be sacred in itself since it is only a tool to stop the mind in order to open it to what is truly sacred. However, an esoteric Christian may perfer to use as a focal point a cross, a picture of Christ, or some other Christian symbol. Christian mantras, such as the Lord's Prayer or the Rosary with its repetitions of the "Hail Mary," may be used as well. St. Francis sometimes prayed simply by repeating the name "Jesus."

The idea is to stop the ordinary movements of the mind in order to reach the mind of God. Let the mind take a vacation from ordinary thought and discover what happens. Don't expect anything; just let it be. In meditation, splendid ideas and insights may sometimes come, undoubtedly the fruit of cleansing the channels of communication. You need not reject these thoughts; but after acknowledging them, set them aside for the period of meditation and quietly return to the stillness out of which the fresh energy behind all creative thought ultimately flows.

Here is a more active form of practice many Christian meditators find meaningful: Visualize a scene from the Bible—say, the story of one of Jesus' miracles or post-resurrection appearances. Then let go of the visualization and just let the warm light of Christ's love infuse you. Finally, draw your thought to the meaning of this story in terms of your own life experience and consider how you are going to express that meaning after you have finished meditating.

Prayer and meditation ought to be practiced in the same place, and that place should be meaningful to you. It might be a room that has a religious picture or symbol in it and above all is clean and quiet. Noise of course is distracting but can be dealt with if it is from outside, like street or industrial or next-apartment noise. Racket from radios or TVs or telephones or other people in the same area should be avoided. You should find a place and time where you can be assured of privacy for at least fifteen or twenty minutes.

Try to identify a time when, on most days, you will be free for prayer and meditation, can be reasonably sure of not being disturbed, and are at your psychological peak for this activity. If you are a "morning person," get up a few minutes early and set time apart for devotions first thing in the morning. If you are the opposite, the best time might be late afternoon or early evening. Prayer and meditation deserve the best moments of the day.

Finally, what about posture? For some, kneeling is natural for prayer; others prefer to sit in a chair. Meditation may be done seated on the floor in some approximation of the lotus posture of Buddhist monks, but to many Christians, that is too Eastern and exotic; like most of the great Christian mystics of the past, they prefer to meditate kneeling or seated. Keep the body erect in whatever posture you are in, but not so rigid as to produce excessive tension or muscle pain. Do not hesitate to shift slightly if necessary, but avoid fidgeting. In all such practice, the body is meant to be a quiet and well-trained servant, not a master.

If you are like most people, you will find that distractions of thought are far more likely to be a nuisance than any fidgeting of the body. Wandering thoughts will arise, armies of them in full array: fantasies, arguments, memories, worries. Sometimes you will suddenly realize that several minutes of the time you had set apart for prayer and meditation have been lost in such distractions.

Worrying about wandering or obtrusive thoughts only makes things worse. Very few of us can entirely control our thoughts, any more than we can control temptations. When wandering thoughts arise during meditation, don't fight them; resistance only creates tension and is a subtle form of attachment. Instead, simply release the thoughts gently and let them go. I like to use the image of releasing a balloon and watching it rise in the air until it finally disappears from sight. Then return to the prayer or meditation as though the thoughts had never occurred, continuing in this way until the time for the exercise is over.[4]

After meditating is the time to practice the continual presence of God. On one level it is not easy to say exactly how that is to be done. It should not be just a matter of technique, but something so deeply ingrained that it is more like a habit or a part of one's nature. Practicing the presence of God can be learned with the help of certain techniques, like prayer and meditation, until it begins to seem like the natural state it actually is.

Here are several practices that can help. Say a

prayer or Christian "mantra" under your breath continually, even while you are doing other things. We have suggested a few, such as the Lord's Prayer or the Hail Mary. The Jesus Prayer, "Lord Jesus Christ, Son of God, have mercy on me," may appeal to those who are drawn to the mysticism of Eastern orthodoxy.

Another way is to quietly bless all persons, animals, objects, and situations you encounter. Just say, silently and reverently, "God bless you, friend," or something similar. This practice is especially effective in dealing with persons and occasions that we find difficult. It is a way of creating thought-forms that channel divine grace or energy to the situations of everyday life, above all to those that anger or intimidate us.

A third way is to dedicate all that we do to God. Whether working, playing, parenting, or hanging out with friends—whatever you do in the course of the day—say under your breath, "I'm dedicating this action to God and am doing it in God's service."

A final way is to see God in all whom you meet. Make a special effort to perceive the divine light in each person who comes your way—at home, in the office, in the store, or just on the street or at the mall. Perceiving people's inner divinity will help bring it forward to their own consciousness as well, so treat them like the gods in the making that they are. No less, see the divine presence in all animals and everything else: the trees, the sun, the moon, the wind, the hardness of tables and chairs, the softness of blankets. All things are God's masquerade and it is a great spiritual game to detect where God is hidden—everywhere!

These ways of practicing the presence are not mutually exclusive. Several can be done at once, though different people may have particular preferences. The important thing is to carry the meditational mind into the world, subtly combining it with the practical, working mind. We need to be amphibians, living in both the divine and the workaday worlds at the same time. It can be done, and this is what the pilgrimage is all about.

This thought brings us to the issues of the ultimate multi-dimensional nature of our quest and where we are going from where we are right now, between birth and death in this world.

8

Traveling into a Far Country: Life, Death, and the Other Side of Death

We have all attended funerals, perhaps even recently. Almost inevitably, the occasion gives rise to deep reflection. The passing of someone about whom we care inevitably leads us to think about human life, both theirs and ours, in the largest possible context—that of the universe and infinite reality itself. At the same time, the experience brings our minds back to the particulars of a life which make it unique, heartwarming, and unforgettable. In the Buddhist scriptures we are told that all is interconnected, like a jeweled net or web in which each person uniquely links or reflects the universe from a particular angle and sends a special influence to the whole over fine but firm lines to the ends of space and time. The universe without a particular person—without, say, Uncle Joe's or Aunt Sue's distinctive smile and way of talking—would have been a quite different universe from the one we know, and a lesser one. And from now on, life will reflect their influence, through fellow workers, students, business associates, loved ones, children, and their children's children, far into the future.

The Scriptures of the Christian faith tell us that death has no sting and the grave no victory. Although beliefs about the life of the world to come vary, all of us can affirm that the beauty, gifts, and wisdom of an individual life are always a victory, and its ending a time of sorrow as well as of thankfulness and happy remembrance. The universe which manifested this person could never be considered impersonal or meaningless.

The classical Christian tradition, above all in its esoteric interpretations, says still more in the Nicene Creed:

> . . . And we believe in one holy catholic and apostolic church. We acknowledge one baptism for the remission of sins. And we look for the resurrection of the dead and the life of the world to come. Amen. (Liberal Catholic version)

These resounding last words of the Nicene Creed, recognized as authoritative by the majority of Christians, make awesome assertions about things past, present, and to come.

The word *catholic* actually means "for all." Far from implying a narrow, sectarian view of the church, it actually signifies that there is a spiritual reality to which all souls belong, whether they realize it or not. All illumined souls—past, present, or future, whether in the world of flesh or on the inner planes—are in mystic communion, knowing something of one another's lives and loves. Likewise, "one baptism for the remission of sins" means esoterically that, because we are all parts of the one unity of the living, we can all be reconciled in God. Similarly, the "resurrection of the dead"—in some versions the resurrection of the *body*—declares that divisions between flesh and spirit, between what we call "living" and "dead," are only relative and can be transcended. Death only seems to be final; in actuality, it is life that triumphs.

Christianity is often considered a kind of salvation cult, in which having the right sort of sacramental magic, or the right theological faith, or even the right number of good deeds, can assure a place in heaven instead of hell—religion as fire insurance! The problem with this view is that it is dualistic, making a hard distinction between this life and the next, between heaven and hell, between the saved and the damned. As we have seen, the esoteric outlook instead pushes always toward oneness because it looks inward rather than outward, and the more deeply we press inward behind the surfaces of the world, the more all things converge.

For most of us, death essentially means the absence of our separate individual consciousness through the cessation of the bodily life-support systems that keep it aware. Yet such a cessation is only a flicker of thought away, whether through sleep, fugue, or the end of life as we know it. And it can mean one of two things: either the blank blackness of the end of consciousness, or the absorption of individual consciousness into something far larger, inconceivable to our present understanding.

Esotericism certainly points toward the latter possibility, since it emphasizes that consciousness or spirit is always present in our universe along with matter. And consciousness is ultimately more lasting—that is, life wins in the end—because it is the unity behind the apparent separateness of the world of matter, giving it form even when in our space and time it seems to revert to chaos.

So it is that life and consciousness do not die but are transformed: ". . . we await a Savior, the Lord Jesus Christ, who will change our lowly body to be like his glorious body, by the power which enables him even to subject all things to himself" (Phil. 3: 20-21). In the kingdom of Christ and what he represents, the dualism of life and death are overcome, and life prevails.

Knowing the oneness behind life and death is not easy. It is not always simple to think in each present moment that the moment and we ourselves are eternal, when we see death all around us and sometimes feel it within ourselves. We also live under relative truth and in conditioned reality. This means that we live in space and time, and therein, so it seems, we can live in only one place and one moment at a time. If we are living in New York or Honolulu, we are not also living in Hong Kong. If we are living in the late twentieth century, we are not also living in the first century with Jesus or the twenty-fifth with Buck Rogers. Or so it seems. Conditioned through the finitude of our minds, we do not easily think other than in these particularistic modes; and if we press at their limits, we may seem to be approaching madness as much as unconditioned Reality.

In conditioned consciousness, one thing comes after another: life advances inevitably from infancy to aging to death, and then to whatever comes next, if anything. Because of our conditioned nature, answers to the inevitable question, "What happens to us after we die?" can be put into narrative form by the esoteric tradition.

The beginning of the story can be seen in accounts of near-death experiences, which have become common recently. Typically, a person who has been declared clinically "dead" and then resuscitated reports having had certain impressions during that time. There might be a sense of separation from the physical body, so that it is seen from above, as though the subject were floating at the top of the hospital room and looking down dispassionately on his or her body. There might come a rushing feeling, as though one were racing through a dark tunnel toward bright, beautiful light. Some report meeting a "Being of Light" who exudes accepting and overflowing love, or one may experience a "life review" that can be less pleasant. At this point, most of those who are returning to their bodies are sent or choose to come back, although a few may linger to see the green fields and splendid mountains of the other side.

In some cases the experience is not as agreeable. On occasion dark demonic entities obstruct the passage between the worlds. Some have seen ominous red lights, or sinister grinding wheels, or perhaps most terrible of all, nothing but an endless void suggesting utter loneliness and meaninglessness. We can not simply correlate the quality of the experience with the character of the experiencer—those who have good experiences are not measurably better people than those whose experiences are negative. In either case—although perhaps especially when it was good experience—the episode is unforgettable for those who have returned from it. It often leads to profound changes in faith, attitude, and way of life. Some report that they have lost all fear of death, have become more loving of all beings, and now possess a deep, though virtually inexpressible, understanding of the mystery and meaning of existence.

The exact nature of these near-death experiences remains a mystery. Nonetheless, they can serve as a parable of the esoteric understanding of life after death[1] which tells us that at physical death the etheric body first detaches itself from the dying body of flesh. This would correlate with the experience of floating in the room, above the physical form. Then the etheric body falls away, leaving the astral body along with the mental and higher principles. This emergence on the astral plane would be similar to the passage through the dark tunnel to the place where beings of light dwell. But this place is also the home of potentially frightening lower astral entities, made what it is in part by the thought-forms of each entity in it.

After the desires and attachments carried over from life have been exhausted in the astral plane, the astral body is shed and the departed person enters Devachan, the heaven-world of the mental plane.

This transition is called the "second death," and that term suggests something of its finality. Thereafter, there are no conscious memories, no particular attachments, and no continuity in any ordinary sense linking the entity with the previous earthly life. Subtle karmic impressions remain that are sufficient to determine a person's overall character and concerns and later to determine the conditions under which a person is reborn. But to the mind now enjoying the splendor of Devachan, the impetus is entirely forward. Thoughts are slowly gathering that will furnish the ideas and themes for the life to come. When this process is finally finished, a womb will be found through which this being will be born again, until it is ready to leave behind the karmic need for expression in physical form altogether.

Although mainstream Christianity does not accept a doctrine of reincarnation, it should be noted that reincarnation as it was just described does not appear to be inconsistent with Christian experience. Rewards and punishments are certainly handed out on the astral plane. The concept of second-death is compatible with the insistence of conventional Christianity that a person born into this world is *like* a new creation; she or he ordinarily possesses no memories, talents, or conspicuous behavior patterns that would identify them as the reincarnation of anyone's Aunt Sue or Uncle Joe or any other particular person.

On the other hand, even Christians must presumably deal with the question of why people are born in widely varying circumstances, some far more advantageous than others. To explain it as God's will is hardly an adequate answer. Christians—especially those who consider themselves esoteric Christians with some insight into the secret wisdom—should not hesitate to reflect on this question. The reasons for the conditions of one's birth are connected with the unfinished business and unfulfilled dreams of earlier lives.

In the end, the ultimate purpose is that all things may be fulfilled, all works completed, and all dreams finished, so that Christ may be all and in all (Col. 3:11). Finishing the dream that is in each of us, playing it out through life after life in all its glory, is part of that grand pattern of interacting dreams that is the mind of Christ.

Let this, then, be the meaning of esoteric Christianity: that it not only sees Christianity as the most dramatic and romantic of religions, but that it also dreams the greatest dreams of any religion and holds that dreams are real, the essences of which all worlds are made.

APPENDIX I:
THE INNER PLANES

This explanation is for the benefit of readers who may not be familiar with the concept of the inner planes referred to in this book.

The Theosophical interpretation of the esoteric wisdom demarcates several "inner planes" within a human being and in the universe as a whole. They are the physical plane; the astral or feeling plane; the mental plane; the intuitive plane; and the divine within. The individual and the universal astral and mental planes are distinct yet intersect and interact on deep levels, just as do one's physical body and the physical universe as a whole. These inner planes fill up, as it were, the continuum between the individual in the physical body and the God-level of universal divine reality.

The use of the word *planes* is, of course, only a metaphor, as are other terms sometimes employed, such as *sheaths* or *spheres*. They are not actually one inside the other like a Russian babushka doll, but interpenetrate or coexist in the same space at the same time, just as oxygen can exist in water and water in a sponge because of the varying degrees of fineness of matter. A fundamental premise of our approach, then, is that reality is multilayered just as Jesus knew it to be. Just as the skin, flesh, and bones of a physical body are all equally real, so are the physical, emotional, mental, intuitive, and purely conscious levels of existence.

Three points are important about this schema.

First, all levels are made up of matter, although the inner planes are made of much finer gradations than what we ordinarily think of as material. Second, all levels are also aspects of consciousness, for consciousness is always part and parcel of matter in the manifested world as we know it, like the front and back of the same head. The ratio, so to speak, may vary: a brain has more consciousness proportionate to its matter than a stone, and an angel even more than a human brain. But the important point is that everything has some of both; they are not two separate realities forever distinct from one another like land and sea, but rather are interwoven, as the human body consists of both sea-water and air-breathing mortal clay. Matter gives consciousness form, and both are in a great continuum. Finally, these planes exist not only within a human being; the esoteric tradition insists they are universal, though they may manifest in a humanly understandable way within human experience. Theosophy teaches that we came out of worlds that emphasize astral, mental, and intuitive realities just as our present world emphasizes the physical. We will pass back into the astral and mental realms after physical death and return there again in much later stages of evolution to deal with our unfinished business there, just as we move now from day to night and night to day.

The esoteric Christian model describes seven principles existing within each person and, by correlation, within the universe as a whole. They are divided into a lower quaternity—the physical body and the three inner planes just mentioned—and a higher

Trinity of God as Father, Son, and Holy Spirit.

The lower quaternity begins with the physical body. In esoteric teaching, it includes not only the body made up of its solid, liquid, and gaseous parts, but also the etheric sphere surrounding the body, composed of matter still finer than gases, similar to the bioenergtic or bioelectric field surrounding the body known to science. In esoteric teaching the etheric sphere provides a mold or model for the body. It is the vehicle of life energy, and separates from the body at death, bearing the higher planes with it and dissolving soon after. Occasionally an etheric shell, or fragments thereof, may survive longer, providing one basis for ghost stories.

Next comes the astral or emotional body which is said to be based on desire, but desire that can no sooner desire something than it appears—as an astral apparition made by mind-force. Many of our dreams and fantasies, both sleeping and waking, are astral plane activities. Discarnate beings on the astral plane can and do interact with them, infecting us with desires and providing opportunities for their fulfillment in dreams and fantasies, or even in out-of-body experiences. Though most astral thought and astral-plane beings are needy in some way, requiring our healing compassion, not all that is on the astral level should be thought of as bad; great works of creativity can come out of the highest reaches of the astral plane.

The mental body is thought on a more refined level than the astral, comprised not of desire-based thoughts, but rather thoughts that are the seeds of creativity and grand in scope, encompassing vast ranges of understanding. The after-death state called Devachan is on the mental plane; here entities rest and, on the basis of karma, gather seed-thoughts that will provide the deep motifs of their next lives. Devachan corresponds to the common idea of heaven.

At a deeper level is the intuitive plane, of which little can be said. It is formless thought just beginning to find itself, like the babble of infants, discovering joy in its being and its separate identity and in the wordless wonder of perceiving shapes and movement for the first time. Flashes of intuitive insight, which are the sources of creativity as well as occasions of deep joy, have their roots in this plane.

The inner trinity consists of the divine spirit, the monad, and the atma. The divine spirit is the personal expression of the Holy Spirit, the Lord and giver of life, energy, and vitality. The monad, corresponding to the Logos, is the pilgrim self experiencing many forms and planes, giving form and wisdom to our temporal experiences. The atma is God the Father within. To know the atma as God and as our own true nature is the supreme object of the spiritual quest.

These inner planes are stages of our own involution and evolution. We came through intuitive, mental, and astral worlds before arriving in this physical one, and so they are part of our deep background and heritage; we will evolve back through those worlds, experiencing them in a rich and wondrous way, after our journey on this planet is done. The planes are both part of our after-death experience and are here in the present as well.

Pilgrims on the inner planes are drawn to human worship. Angels, whose natural home is the heavenly mental level, come to bathe in the light of love and grace generated by the gestures of worship and the powerful energies of love and peace that are raised like domes of light by effective worship. These angels help to spread grace through the congregation and out into the surrounding area and the world.

Astral entities may also be drawn to worship, though they are entities more in need of help than able to assist. These are departed souls who are still confused or unable to escape their own ego and its attachment-based desires, and so they are not ready to enter Devachan. They may be earth-bound spirits unable to let go of a place or person that had been traumatically important in their lives. Or they may be attached to gross desires such as for drink or sex and still try vicariously to enjoy them by entering alcoholics or lechers who are living. At higher levels, they may still be preoccupied by ambition or sociability or love of aesthetic beauty, which they can fulfill in the astral plane by making and unmaking worlds to suit their fancies as freely as one does in dream. At the highest levels of the astral plane may be found great artists and musicians or philosophers whose work is still ego-centered. They have not yet exhausted the ego-nature adequately to undergo the "second death," which entails letting go of ego as we know it so that one can enter Devachan and through deep new thoughts sow the seeds of the next life.

Astral beings can be happy, yet they also know on some deep level (as do most of us) that they are imprisoned by their own minds and by their ceaselessly grinding passions and desires, however lofty. Like us, they sense that somewhere is a divine grace or nature that would have the power, if they could only catch a glimpse of its beauty, to distract their thoughts from themselves and so lead them out of the prison of ego. Angelic teachers of power and beauty are found on the astral plane, led there out of a selfless desire to help. Astral beings can also feel drawn to human worship in their earnest desire for aid. Or they may be drawn for less noble reasons, if the worship is debased or if the being is one who finds in religion a suitable means to gratify the lust for power and authority. In our own worship, we need to remember them, pray for them, and speak to them with words of love and welcome.

Christians consider Jesus to be the supreme image in the world of the nature of God and Ultimate Reality, as though he were particularly "transparent" to all that is invisible behind the visible surfaces of earth—"all things visible and invisible," in the words of the Nicene Creed. It is said that Jesus the Christ is both "True God" and "True Man," two persons in one substance, as though he made especially clear in his own person the multilayered realities within which we dwell. The spirits, including those who came from the lower reaches of the astral realm, recognized who he was. At the beginning of his ministry, when he was healing a man who had an unclean spirit, the demon cried out with a loud voice, "What have you to do with us, Jesus of Nazareth? Have you come to destroy us? I know who you are, the Holy One of God" (Luke 4:34).

Jesus found both pain and joy in being so aware of the inner realms and their interconnections, for there are times when knowing too much about the inner side of things makes choices and attitudes difficult. This is knowledge that many people would rather leave alone, preferring one world at a time and keeping to that which is visible to ordinary eyes. Jesus often found himself accused of madness, for the ability to see the multilayered universe hidden to most is hard to distinguish from the delusions of schizophrenia. The only test in the end is not in what is seen, for much of what the mentally ill see may in fact be distorted nightmare versions of the astral plane, but in how one responds to them. Do the demons tear one apart, or does the visionary, like Jesus, master them and go on to become a guide and a shaper of history far surpassing most persons of one-dimensional sight?

Appendix II:
Classics of Christian Spirituality

Here are a few samples of the wealth of mystical and devotional literature found in the Christian tradition. They represent a variety of time periods and Christian traditions. I hope this brief anthology will whet your appetite and lead you to explore more of the fabulous world of spiritual literature related to the Christian faith.

1. The New Testament

What follows is a modern translation of the familiar and much-beloved 13th chapter of St. Paul's First Epistle to the Corinthians:

I may speak with the tongues of men and of angels,
    but if I have no love,
        I am a noisy gong or a clanging cymbal;
I may prophesy, fathom all mysteries and secret lore,
I may have such absolute faith that I can move hills
from their place,
    but if I have no love,
        I count for nothing;
I may distribute all I possess in charity,
I may give up my body to be burnt,
    but if I have no love,
        I make nothing of it.

Love is very patient, very kind. Love knows no jealousy; love makes no parade, gives itself

no airs, is never rude, never selfish, never irri-
tated, never resentful; love is never glad when
others go wrong, love is gladdened by good-
ness, always slow to expose, always eager to
believe the best, always hopeful, always patient.
Love never disappears. As for prophesying, it
will be superseded; as for tongues, they will
cease; as for knowledge, it will be superseded.
For we only know bit by bit, and we only prophesy bit by bit; but when the perfect comes, the
imperfect will be superseded. When I was a
child, I talked like a child, I thought like a child,
I argued like a child; now that I am a man, I am
done with childish ways.

At present we only see the baffling reflections in a mirror,
  but then it will be face to face;
at present I am learning bit by bit,
  but then I shall understand, as all along I have myself
been understood.

Thus "faith and hope and love last on, these three," but
the greatest of all is love.

—James Moffatt, *The Bible, A New Translation* (New York: Harper & Bros., 1922)

2. GNOSTICISM

Esoteric Christians have long appreciated Gnostic literature from the early centuries of Christianity.
Here is a beautiful passage about a mystic dance from
the Gnostic Acts of John (probably 130-150 C.E.):

Now before Jesus was taken . . . gathering

us all together, he said: Before I am handed over
to them, let us hymn the Father, and so go out
to what is waiting. Having bidden us therefore
to make as it were a ring, holding each other's
hands and himself coming in the middle, he
said: Reply with the Amen!

So he began to sing a Hymn and to say,
Glory to Thee, Father! and we, going round in
a circle, said the Amen. Glory to Thee, Word!
Glory to Thee, Grace! Amen. Glory to Thee,
Spirit, Holy One! Glory to Thy Glory! Amen.
We praise Thee, Father, we give Thee thanks,
O light in whom no darkness dwells! Amen.

And for this reason we give thanks: I say, I
will to be saved, and I will to save! Amen. I
will to be freed, and I will to free! Amen. I will
to be wounded [by divine love], and I will to
wound [to give the divine Light to others,
though it may at first be painful]! Amen. I will
to be born, and I will to bear! Amen. I will to
devour [i.e., take the divine into myself], and I
will to be eaten [consumed by the divine]!
Amen. I will to hear, and I will to be heard!
Amen. I will to understand, and I will to be
understood—being all Mind! Amen. I will to
be washed, and I will to wash! Amen.

Grace dances; I will to play on the pipe—
dance, all of you! Amen. I will to mourn—
lament, all of you! Amen. One Ogdoad [di-
vine powers ruling the universe] sings with us!
Amen. The Dodecad [the twelve signs of the
Zodiac] above dances in time! Amen. Whereon

the whole begins to dance! Amen. He who does not dance knows not what is going on! Amen.

I will to flee, and I will to stay! Amen. I will to adorn, and I will to be adorned! Amen. I will to be made one and I will to make one! Amen. I have no house, and I have houses! Amen. I have no place, and I have places! Amen. I have no shrine, and I have shrines! Amen.

I am a Lamp for you who look at me! Amen. I am a Mirror for you who think of me! Amen. I am a Door to you who knock at me! Amen. I am a Way for you, a wayfarer! Amen.

Now respond to my dancing; see thyself in me as I speak, and seeing what I do keep silence on my mysteries. He who dances understands what I am doing, for thine is this passion of the Man which I am about to suffer. For thou couldst not wholly realise what I suffer, had not I, a Word, come to thee from the Father. Seeing what I suffer, thou hast seen me as suffering, and seeing, thou didst not stand firm but wast altogether moved. Hadst thou known how to suffer, thou shouldst have been able not to suffer; then know how to suffer, and thou wilt be able not to suffer. . . .

Having danced these things with us, the Lord went out . . . and when he was hung to the bush [symbolizing the flaming bush from which Moses heard the voice of God] of the Cross, darkness came on over all the land.

—Duncan Greenlees, *The Gospel of the Gnostics* (Adyar, Madras, India: Theosophical Publishing House, 1958). Notes and parentheses omitted.

3. THE CONFESSIONS OF ST. AUGUSTINE

Here one of the great Fathers and theologians of the church describes the inner meaning of his quest for God. Beginning with the famous words, "You have made us for yourself, O Lord, and our hearts are restless till they find their rest in thee," he continues :

I was admonished by all this to return to my own self, and, with you to guide me, I entered into the innermost part of myself, and I was able to do this because you were my helper. I entered and I saw with my soul's eye (such as it was) an unchangeable light shining above this light of my soul and above my mind. It was not the ordinary light which is visible to all flesh, nor something of the same sort, only bigger, as though it might be our ordinary light shining much more brightly and filling everything with its greatness. No, it was not like that; it was different, entirely different from anything of the kind. Nor was it above my mind as oil floats on water or as the heaven is above the earth. It was higher than I, because it made me, and I was lower because I was made by it. He who knows truth knows that light, and he who knows that light knows eternity. Love knows it. O eternal truth and true love and beloved eternity! You are my God; to you I sigh by day and by night. And when I first knew you, you raised me up so that I could see that there is something to see and that I still lacked the ability to see it. And you beat back the weakness of my sight, blazing upon me with your rays, and I trembled in love and in dread, and I found that I was far distant from you, in a region of total unlikeness, as if I were hearing your voice from on high saying, "I am the food of grown men. Grow and you shall feed upon me. And you will not, as with the food of the body, change me into yourself, but you will be changed into me! . . ."

Late it was that I loved You, beauty so ancient and so new, late I loved You! And look, You were within me and I was outside, and there I sought for you and in my ugliness I plunged into the beauties that you have made. You were with me and I was not with you. Those outer beauties kept me from you, yet if they had not been in you, they would not have existed at all. You called, you cried out, you shattered my deafness: you breathed fragrance, and I drew in my breath and I pant for you! I tasted and I am hungry and thirsty: you touched me, and I burned for your peace.

—Mary T. Clark, trans., *Augustine of Hippo: Selected Writings* (New York: Paulist Press, 1984)

4. Medieval Mysticism

In 1373, Julian of Norwich, one the greatest of Christian mystical writers, described in this way one of the showings of divine love that God bestowed upon her:

> "God, of Thy Goodness, give me Thyself; —only in Thee I have all."

In this same time our Lord shewed me a ghostly [spiritual] sight of His homely loving.

I saw that He is to us everything that is good and comfortable for us: He is our clothing that for love wrappeth us, claspeth us, and all encloseth us for tender love, that He may never leave us; being to us all-thing that is good, as to mine understanding.

Also in this He shewed me a little thing, the quantity of an hazelnut, in the palm of my hand; and it was as round as a ball. I looked thereupon with the eye of my understanding, and thought: *What may this be?* and it was answered generally thus: *It is all that is made.* I marvelled how it might last, for methought it might suddenly have fallen to naught for little[ness]. And I was answered in my understanding: *It lasteth, and ever shall [last] for that God loveth it.* And so All-thing hath the Being by the love of God.

In this Little Thing I saw three properties. The First is that God made it, the second is that God loveth it, the third, that God keepeth it. But what is to me verily the Maker, the Keeper, and the Lover—I cannot tell; for till I am Substantially oned [united] to Him, I may never have full rest nor very bliss: that is to say, till I be so fastened to Him, that there is right naught that is made betwixt my God and me.

    —Grace Warrack, ed., *Revelations of Divine Love Recorded by Julian Anchoress of Norwich* A.D., *1373* (London: Methuen, 1901, 1909)

5. Classical Protestantism

Martin Luther, the great Reformation leader, presents these important words about faith, the forgiveness of sins, and the doing of good works out of the power of faith and forgiveness:

Where Christ and faith are not present, here there is no forgiveness of sins or hiding of sins. On the contrary, here there is the sheer imputation and condemnation of sins. Thus God wants to glorify His son, and He Himself wants to be glorified in us through Him.

When we have taught faith in Christ this way, then we also teach about good works. Because you have taken hold of Christ by faith, through whom you are righteous, you should now go and love God and your neighbor. Call upon God, give thanks to Him, preach Him, praise Him, confess Him. Do good to your neighbor, and serve him; do your duty. These are truly good works, which glow from this faith and joy conceived in the heart because we have the forgiveness of sins freely through Christ.

Then whatever there is of cross or suffering to be borne later on is easily sustained. For the yoke that Christ lays upon us is sweet, and His burden is light (Matt. 11:30). When sin has been forgiven and the conscience has been liberated from the burden and the sting of sin, then a Christian can bear everything easily. Because everything within is sweet and pleasant, he willingly does and suffers everything. But when a man goes along in his own righteousness, then whatever he does and suffers is painful and tedious for him, because he is doing it unwillingly.

Therefore we define a Christian as follows: A Christian is not someone who has no sin or feels no sin; he is someone to whom, because of his faith in Christ, God does not impute his sin. This doctrine brings firm consolation to troubled consciences amid genuine terrors. It is not in vain, therefore, that so often and so diligently we inculcate the doctrine of the forgiveness of sins and of the imputation of righteousness for the sake of Christ, as well as the doctrine that a Christian does not have anything to do with the Law and sin, especially in a time of temptation. For to the extent that he is a Christian, he is above the Law and sin, because in his heart he has Christ, the Lord of the Law, as a ring has a gem. Therefore when the Law accuses and sin troubles, he looks to Christ; and when he has taken hold of Him by faith, he has present with him the Victor over the Law, sin, death, and the devil—the Victor whose rule over all these prevents them from harming him.

—Jaroslav Pelikan, ed., *Luther's Works, Vol. 26: Lectures on Galatians, 1535* (Saint Louis: Concordia Publishing House, 1963)

6. QUAKERISM

In this passage from his journals, George Fox, founder of the Society of Friends, or Quakers, presents the themes of the priesthood, or equality, of all believers of the Inner Light that is the true guide of those who follow it, based on his openings, or revelations:

Now after I had received that opening from the Lord, that to be bred at Oxford or Cambridge was not sufficient to fit a man to be a minister of Christ, I regarded the priests less and looked more after the dissenting people. And among them I saw there was some tenderness and many of them came afterwards to be convinced, for they had some openings. But as I had forsaken all the priests, so I left the separate preachers also, and those called the most experienced people; for I saw there was none among them all that could speak to my condition. And when all my hopes in them and in all men was gone, so that I had nothing outwardly to help me, nor could tell what to do, then, O! then I heard a voice which said, There is one, even Christ Jesus, that can speak to thy condition. And when I heard it, my heart did leap for joy. Then the Lord did let me see why there was none upon the earth that could speak to my condition, namely, that I might give Him all the glory. For all are concluded under sin and shut up in unbelief, as I had been, that Jesus Christ might have the pre-eminence, who enlightens and gives grace and faith and power. Thus, when God doth work, who shall let it? And this I know experimentally. My desires after the Lord grew stronger, and zeal in the pure knowledge of God and of Christ alone, without the help of any man, book, or writing. For though I read the Scriptures that spake of Christ and of God, yet I knew Him not but by revelation, as he who hath the key did open, and as the Father of Life drew me to his son by his Spirit. And then the Lord did gently lead me along and did let me see his love, which was endless and eternal, and surpasses all the knowledge that men have in the natural state, or can get by history or books.

—*Passages from the Life and Writings of George Fox, Taken from his Journal* (Philadelphia: Friends Book-Store, 1881)

7. THE ANGLICAN CHURCH

Here are some prayers from *The Book of Common Prayer:*

Almighty God, unto whom all hearts are open, all desires known, and from whom no secrets are hid; Cleanse the thoughts of our hearts by the inspiration of thy Holy Spirit, that we may perfectly love thee, and worthily magnify thy holy Name; through Christ our Lord. Amen.

O Lord Jesus Christ, who saidst unto thine Apostles, Peace I leave with you, my peace I give unto you; Regard not our sins, but the faith of thy Church; and grant to it that peace and unity which is according to thy will, who livest and reignest with the Father and the Holy Ghost, one god, world without end. Amen.

O God, who declarest thy almighty power chiefly in showing mercy and pity; Mercifully grant unto us such a measure of thy grace, that we, running the way of thy commandments, may obtain thy gracious promises, and be made partakers of thy heavenly treasure; through Jesus Christ our Lord. Amen.

Stir up, we beseech thee, O Lord, the wills of thy faithful people; that they, plenteously bringing forth the fruit of good works, may by thee be plenteously rewarded; through Jesus Christ our Lord. Amen.

—*The Book of Common Prayer . . . According to the Use of the Protestant Episcopal Church in the United States of America* (1928 version, Greenwich, CT: Seabury Press, 1953)

8. EASTERN ORTHODOXY

The following passages are from a great nineteenth-century classic of Russian spiritual literature, *The Way of a Pilgrim.* It purports to tell, in the first person, the story of a wandering pilgrim who made his way across that vast land seeking to learn the secret of how to pray without ceasing. His spiritual practice was based on teachings from the *Philokalia*, an anthology of writings from the Eastern church fathers, to which he is here introduced.

By the grace of God I am a Christian man, by my actions a great sinner, and by calling a homeless wanderer of the humblest birth who roams from place to place. My worldly goods are a knapsack with some dried bread in it on my back, and in my breast-pocket a Bible. And that is all.

On the 24th Sunday after Pentecost I went to church to say my prayers there during the Liturgy. The first Epistle of St. Paul to the Thessalonians was being read, and among other words I heard these—"Pray without ceasing." It was this text, more than any other, which forced itself upon my mind, and I began to think how it was possible to pray without ceasing, since a man has to concern himself with other things also in order to make a living. I looked at my Bible, and with my own eyes read the words which I had heard, i.e., that we ought always, at all times and in all places, to pray with uplifted hands. I thought and thought, but knew not what to make of it. "What ought I to do?" I thought. "Where shall I find someone to explain it to me? I will go to the churches where famous preachers are to be heard; perhaps there I shall hear something which will throw light on it for me." I did so. I heard a number of very fine sermons on prayer; what prayer is, how much we need it, and what its fruits are; but no one said how one could succeed in prayer. I heard a sermon on spiritual prayer, and unceasing prayer, but how it was to be done was not pointed out.

[The pilgrim finally found a wise old monk who taught him the secret of prayer.]

"Come in," said he; "I will give you a volume of the holy Fathers from which with God's help you can learn about prayer clearly and in detail."

We went into his cell and he began to speak as follows:

"The continuous interior Prayer of Jesus is a constant uninterrupted calling upon the divine Name of Jesus with the lips, in the spirit, in the heart; while forming a mental picture of

His constant presence, and imploring His grace, during every occupation, at all times, in all places, even during sleep. The appeal is couched in these terms, 'Lord Jesus Christ, have mercy on me.' One who accustoms himself to this appeal experiences as a result so deep a consolation and so great a need to offer the prayer always, that he can no longer live without it, and it will continue to voice itself within him of its own accord. Now do you understand what prayer without ceasing is?"

"Yes indeed, Father, and in God's name teach me how to gain the habit of it," I cried, filled with joy.

"Read this book," he said. "It is called *The Philokalia*, and it contains the full and detailed science of constant interior prayer, set forth by twenty-five holy Fathers. The book is marked by a lofty wisdom and is so profitable to use that it is considered the foremost and best manual of the contemplative spiritual life. As the revered Nicephorus said, 'It leads one to salvation without labour and sweat.'"

"Is it then more sublime and holy than the Bible?" I asked.

"No, it is not that, but it contains clear explanations of what the Bible holds in secret and which cannot be easily grasped by our short-sighted understanding. I will give you an illustration. The sun is the greatest, the most resplendent and the most wonderful of heavenly luminaries, but you cannot contemplate and examine it simply with unprotected eyes. You have to use a piece of artificial glass which is many millions of times smaller and darker than the sun. But through this little piece of glass you can examine the magnificent monarch of stars, delight in it, and endure its fiery rays. Holy Scripture also is a dazzling sun, and this book *The Philokalia* is the piece of glass which we use to enable us to contemplate the sun in its imperial splendour. Listen now, I am going to read you the sort of instruction it gives on unceasing interior prayer."

He opened the book, found the instruction by St. Simeon the New Theologian, and read: "Sit down alone and in silence. Lower your head, shut your eyes, breathe out gently and imagine yourself looking into your own heart. Carry your mind, i.e., your thoughts, from your head to your heart. As you breathe out, say 'Lord Jesus Christ, have mercy on me.' Say it moving your lips gently, or simply say it in your mind. Try to put all other thoughts aside. Be calm, be patient, and repeat the process very frequently."

—R.M. French, trans., *The Way of a Pilgrim* (New York: Harper & Bros., 1930, 1952)

9. ROMAN CATHOLICISM

These passages by the great convert to Roman Catholicism, John Henry Newman, describe the spitirual appeal of Catholic worship and devotion as

presented in fictionalized form in his novel of con-
version, *Loss and Gain*:

> [T]he Catholic Church alone is beautiful.
> You would see what I mean if you went into a
> foreign cathedral, or even into one of the Catho-
> lic churches in our large towns. The celebrant,
> deacon, and subdeacon, acolytes with lights, the
> incense, and the chanting—all combine to one
> end, one act of worship. You feel it *is* really a
> worshipping; every sense, eyes, ears, smell, are
> made to know that worship is going on. The
> laity on the floor saying their beads, or making
> their acts; the choir singing out the *Kyrie*; and
> the priest and his assistant bowing low, and say-
> ing the *Confiteor* to each other. This is worship,
> and it is far above reason. . . .
> What particularly struck him [Charles, the
> prospective convert] was, that whereas in the
> Church of England the clergyman or the organ
> was everything and the people nothing, except
> so far as the clerk is their representative, here
> it was just reversed. The priest hardly spoke,
> or at least audibly; but the whole congregation
> was as though one vast instrument or
> Panharmonicon, moving all together, and what
> was most remarkable, as if self-moved. They
> did not seem to require any one to prompt or
> direct them, though in the Litany the choir took
> the alternate parts. The words were in Latin,
> but every one seemed to understand them thor-
> oughly, and to be offering up his prayers to the

Blessed Trinity, and the Incarnate Savior, and the great Mother of God, and the glorified Saints, with hearts full in proportion to the energy of the sounds they uttered. . . . it is the working of one Spirit in all, making many one.

While he was thus thinking, a change came over the worship. A priest, or at least an assistant, had mounted for a moment above the altar, and removed a chalice or vessel which stood there; he could not see distinctly. A cloud of incense was rising on high; the people suddenly all bowed low; what could it mean? The truth flashed on him, fearfully yet sweetly; it was the Blessed Sacrament—it was the Lord Incarnate who was on the altar, who had come to visit and to bless His people. It was the Great Presence, which makes a Catholic Church different from every other place in the world; which makes it as no other place can be, holy . . . he threw himself on the pavement, in sudden self-abasement and joy. . . .

[A few days later] It was Sunday morning about seven o'clock, and Charles had been admitted into the communion of the Catholic Church about an hour since. He was still kneeling in the church of the Passionists before the Tabernacle, in the possession of a deep peace and serenity of mind, which he had not thought possible on earth. It was more like the stillness which almost sensibly affects the ears, when a bell which had long been tolling stops, or when a vessel, after much tossing at sea, finds itself in harbor. It was such as to throw him back in memory on his earliest years, as if he were really beginning life again. But there was more than the happiness of childhood in his heart; he seemed to feel a rock under his feet; it was the *soliditas Cathedrae Petri* [solidarity with the chair of Peter]. He went on kneeling, as if he were already in Heaven, with the throne of God before him, and Angels around; and as if to move were to lose his privilege.

    —John Henry Newman, *Loss and Gain; or, the Story of a Convert* (Boston: Patrick Donahoe, 1854)

10. LIBERAL CATHOLICISM

Here Geoffrey Hodson, a well-known priest of the Liberal Catholic Church who was widely believed to have had gifts of clairvoyance, relates his inner perceptions of a service of Procession and Benediction of the Blessed Sacrament, the latter being the same service described above by Newman in a Roman Catholic setting. Hodson was at St. Michael's Liberal Catholic Church in Huizen, the Netherlands.

The commencement of the procession at the altar is a signal to the heavenly hosts, who gather in thousands to wait upon and to reverence the passing of the Body of the Lord. As the beam shines forth in all its splendour, it seems to cleave a passage through all the worlds from the spiritual to the physical, opening a way for the descent of the power of the higher planes. In their subtler bodies the officiants repeat plane by plane the physical procession, and the angels of each level of the inner worlds participate. They hover relatively motionless above the garden and grounds through which the procession passes. Their bodies make a wonderful chalice of light which they offer to the angelic Logos of our system to be filled with His life which, passing through them, fills the earth and all the people of the earth with the power, the beauty and the blessing of the angelic host. Great Archangels pause in their mighty cosmic tasks to utilize the occasion for a downpouring of their blessing. Special shining ones, white and glorious, attached to the great work of the Church of St. Michael, themselves descend and link their power with that of the bishop who holds the Host aloft.

As the great prayer is recited:

> To the most holy and adorable trinity, Father, Son and Holy Spirit, three Persons in one God; to Christ our Lord, the only wise counsellor, the Prince of Peace; to the seven mighty Spirits before the throne; and to the glorious Assembly of just men made perfect, the Watchers, the Saints, the Holy Ones, be praise unceasing from every living creature; and honour, might and glory, henceforth and for evermore. Amen.

A six-armed cross of light is formed, with the Host as its living heart, one arm reaches high up into the heavens, its opposite arm into the earth beneath, the other four to each of the quarters of the globe. Through each arm the appropriate power is conveyed, the heavenly forces descend, the mighty powers from the centre of the planet arise and a great representative of each of the regents of the North, East, South and West assembles the hosts of his angelic order along the line of his respective arm. Numbers of nature spirits from the surrounding country—gnomes, elves, fairies and sylphs, lesser and greater angels, come in great multitudes to join their human brethren in their worship and adoration of the Lord, and at the *Ascription* a mighty torrent of life and power flashes up into the intuitional world from all the surrounding earth, the plants, the trees, and from all the hearts and minds of human and angelic worshippers. Even the birds seem to sing more sweetly and with a greater joy as the procession passes through the gardens in which they live. There is a great release of power from all physical manifestations within the area of the direct influence of the service.

Down comes the wondrous response from on high, and all the earth is refreshed. A new life flows through all forms as if every atom were vivified and quickened by the great descent of power. At the supreme moment, when the *Host* is elevated, the angels seem awed into silence and hushed stillness; the revelation of the power and the majesty of the Lord of Love is so marvellous that even they—incarnations of life, light and motion—become still. Reverently they adore his manifestation on earth; solemnly they worship him. From every human heart love, adoration and worship pour forth into the Heart of Love in which the whole world is embraced.

 —Geoffrey Hodson, *Clairvoyant Investigations of Christian Origins and Ceremonial* (London and Ojai, CA: St. Alban Press, 1977)

Notes

Preface

1. The best book for studying the Grail legends in the spirit of esoteric Christianity is by John Matthews and Marian Green *The Grail Seeker's Companion* (Wellingborough, England: Aquarian Press, 1986). See also Gareth Knight, *The Secret Tradition in Arthurian Legend* (Wellingborough, England: Aquarian Press, 1984); A.E. Waite, *The Hidden Church of the Holy Grail* (London: Rebman, 1909); and John Matthews, *King Arthur and the Grail Quest* (London: Blandford, 1994).

Chapter 1: What We Are Searching For

1. The expression "thought-forms" represents the Theosophical concept that thoughts are not merely formless, ephemeral ideas, but create distinct energy patterns, called thought-forms, that persist and can cause effects on subtle planes of awareness.
2. See my description of the pilgrim stages of a single life from infancy to old age in *The Pilgrim Self* (Wheaton, IL: Quest Books, 1996).

Chapter 2: The Holy Trinity:
Christian Meaning in the Three Outpourings of Creation

1. See Annie Besant, *Esoteric Christianity*, abridged ed. (Wheaton, IL: Quest Books, 1982), 185. Originally published by the Theosophical Publishing House in 1901.

Chapter 3: Jesus and the Never-Ending Story:
From Eden to Eternity

1. *Monad* is a Theosophical term for the ultimate indivisible spiritual entity or spark of the divine. It is ageless, infinite,

and boundless; monads are innumerable, individual centers of consciousness.

2. The Liberal Catholic Church is an independent old Catholic body that is neither Roman Catholic nor Protestant. Although it is historically Christian in outlook, it combines traditional ritual with a deeply mystical practice. Some Liberal Catholics have also been Theosophists.

CHAPTER 4: IF I BE LIFTED UP: ALTARS OF THE HEART

1. Annie Besant and C. W. Leadbeater, *Thought-Forms*, abridged ed. (Wheaton, IL: Theosophical Publishing House, 1969). Originally published in 1901.

2. C. W. Leadbeater, *The Science of the Sacraments* (1920; reprint, Adyar, Madras, India: Theosophical Publishing House, 1988).

3. Ibid., 77-79.

4. Ibid., 83fn.

5. C. W. Leadbeater, *The Hidden Side of Things* (1913; reprint, Adyar, Madras, India: Theosophical Publishing House, 1974), 163-166. Reprinted in *The Science of the Sacraments*, 212-215.

CHAPTER 5: TWO OR THREE GATHERED TOGETHER:
THE NATURE OF CHRISTIAN COMMUNITY

1. The word translated as "spider" is sometimes rendered "lizard."

2. C. W. Leadbeater, *Invisible Helpers* (Adyar, Madras, India: Theosophical Publishing House, 1928), 1.

CHAPTER 6: A LITTLE CHILD: CHRISTIAN ETHICS

1. Cited in Morris Bishop, *The Middle Ages* (Boston: Houghton Mifflin, 1987), 77.

2. On vegetarianism and reasons for it, see John Robbins, *Diet for a New America* (Walpole, NH: Stillpoint, 1987). On parallels between raising animals for meat or service and human slavery, the following is a powerful and disturbing work:

Marjorie Spiegel, *The Dreaded Comparison* (New York: Mirror Books, 1988).

3. On this aspect of a Christian argument for vegetarianism and animal rights, see Andrew Linzey, *Animal Theology* (Urbana: University of Illinois Press, 1995).

4. This theme runs through much of Reinhold Niebuhr's work. See, for example, "The Morality of Nations," chapter 4 in *Moral Man and Immoral Society* (New York: Scribner, 1932).

CHAPTER 7: A GREAT WHILE BEFORE DAWN: PRAYER, MEDITATION, AND SPIRITUAL LIFE

1. R. M. French, trans., *The Way of the Pilgrim* (New York: Harper & Bros., 1930, 1952). See page 134.

2. There are many versions of the *Book of Common Prayer* of the Church of England and its sister churches throughout the world. For citations from one, see Appendix II, Section 7.

3. *Liturgy* of the Liberal Catholic Church (London: St. Alban Press, 1983).

4. For more on meditation, see the author's book, *Finding the Quiet Mind* (Wheaton, Il: Quest Books, 1983).

CHAPTER 8: TRAVELING TO A FAR COUNTRY: LIFE, DEATH, AND THE OTHER SIDE OF DEATH

1. The esoteric view of life after death here presented follows that of modern Theosophy; for a fuller account see Robert Ellwood, *Theosophy* (Wheaton, IL: Quest Books, 1986), 107-14; and James S. Perkins, *Through Death to Rebirth* (Wheaton, IL: Quest Books, 1961, 1982). See also Appendix I of this book.

QUEST BOOKS
are published by
The Theosophical Society in America
Wheaton, Illinois 60189-0270
a branch of a world organization
dedicated to the promotion of the unity of
humanity and the encouragement of the study of
religion, philosophy, and science, to the end that
we may better understand ourselves and our place in
the universe. The Society stands for complete
freedom of individual search and belief.
For further information about its activities,
write, call 1-800-669-1571, or consult its Web page:
http://www. theosophical.org.

*The Theosophical Publishing House
is aided by the generous support of
THE KERN FOUNDATION,
a trust established by Herbert A. Kern
and dedicated to Theosophical education.*